*We wait in darkness! Come, all ye who listen,
help in our night journey.*

IROQUOIS CHANT [1]

For Sally, Aaron and Rebecca

Contents

Introduction

There are three things extremely hard, Steel,
a Diamond, and to know one's self.

BENJAMIN FRANKLIN

I wonder if I've been changed in the night (asks Alice). Let me think was I
the same when I got up this morning? I almost think I can remember feel-
ing a little different. But if I'm not the same, the next question is 'Who in
the world am I?' Ah, that's the great puzzle!

LEWIS CARROLL: Alice in Wonderland

This book is about you. It is about ways of exploring aspects of yourself. If the
health professions are to progress, they must first discover themselves. Caring,
depends upon you knowing more about who you are. Why? Because we cannot help other people until we are a bit clearer about ourselves.

Once we are more self-aware we are better able to give ourselves to others.
We are also more likely to take care of ourselves and we are more likely to know
our strengths and deficits. Once we know those deficits, too, we can start to rec-
tify them. We can also build on our strengths. The worst position of all is being
in the dark about ourselves: knowing neither our good or our bad points. This
book is aimed at helping you to find out more about yourself.

■ HOW IS THIS BOOK ORGANISED?

The book offers a wide range of easy-to-do exersises and activities that help you
to reflect on the question 'Who am I?' and to find some answers to the question.
All of them are easy to do and most of them are enjoyable, if challenging.
Almost all of them you can do on your own. A few need the help of another
person. Some can be carried out in a small group, although this is never essential. You can either work straight through the book or you can do a few exercises at a time from different chapters. One useful way of using the book is to
browse through it and find what catches YOUR eye. It is likely that the exercises that you are first drawn to are ones that have most meaning for you.

One thing is important. Do not *rush* the exercises. It is easy to read through
some of them and think 'Yes, I've got the hang of that'. This misses the point.
All of the exercises encourage you to reflect on what you think, feel or do.
Becoming reflective is part of the process of becoming effective in your job.

1

Reflection takes time. Try not to rush through the book in one sitting. Instead, pick one or two activities and take your time doing them.

I have used nurses and nursing where exercises and examples are given, but these apply equally to all members of the health professions.

Throughout the book you are asked three questions under each of the headings, in each of the chapters. Read the questions and respond by circling one of the following:

Strongly Agree	Agree	Uncertain	Disagree	Strongly Disagree
SA	A	U	D	SD

Again, do not rush through these questions but try to answer them as honestly as possible. Also, try this. First, answer each question *as if you were telling the answer to another person*. Then, answer the question *for yourself*. Notice any difference between the two answers! Alternatively, you may want to compare your answers to these questions to those of a colleague or friend. If you are using this book in a small group it will be useful if you discuss your answers. However, remain conscious of the two possible levels at work: your answers for yourself and your answers for others.

There are many other questions raised throughout the text. The aim, throughout, is to get you to reflect on who you are and what you think. You are not asked to agree with everything that you read, only to consider the degree to which what you are reading makes sense to you.

I have grouped the references together at the end of the book along with various notes to further reading on the topics under discussion. This was to avoid cluttering the text with lots of names and dates. Using this system has also meant that I have been able to add comments about the books referred to in the text. You may want to read the book through first without referring to the reference notes and then return to look up specific names and dates.

■ WHAT IS IN THE BOOK?

The book offers a number of things. First, it contains theory about aspects of self awareness. Second, it offers you the exercises discussed above. Third, it includes a series of checklists that contain a 'shorthand' approach to thinking about aspects of self awareness. Finally, the book ends with an extensive bibliography so that you can read more on the topics that interest you.

Many of the activities in this book will help you in very practical ways. You will learn how to write a better curriculum vitae (CV). You will explore ways of becoming more assertive and ways of coping with stress. Self-awareness is not an airy fairy, abstract concept but a down to earth, practical necessity.

Self-awareness is a lifelong project. In discovering more about ourselves we also discover two important things: how different we are from other people and how similar we are to them. These similarities and differences can help in recognising and responding to the needs of the people we care for.

I hope you will find this book both stimulating and thought-provoking. I hope you won't agree with everything in it but that it will help you sort out what you think and feel about various things. Finally, I hope you *enjoy* doing the exercises. Try not to take them too seriously. You can learn a lot about yourself if you keep a sense of humour and try not to be too earnest about the whole thing. I would be pleased to hear from you if you have any comments to make about any aspect of this book.

1 | The Self

Know then thyself, presume not God to scan.
The proper study of mankind is man.

ALEXANDER POPE

Any life, no matter how long and complex it may be, is made up of a
SINGLE MOMENT – the moment in which a man finds out, once and for
all, who he is.

JORGE LUIS BORGES

Keywords	● Self concept
	● Physical self
	● Ideal self
	● Self-for-others
	● Social self
	● Spiritual self
	● Darker self
	● Sexual self
Aims of this chapter	● To explore the concept of self
	● To identify aspects of the self
	● To relate the concept of self to nursing

■ WHAT IS THE SELF?

Who are you? What are you like? What do other people think of you? All of these are questions about the 'self'. Yet, if we are not careful, the self turns out to be a difficult thing to pin down. We all know what we mean when we talk of ourselves but few of us could ever define exactly what we mean. In this chapter, we explore and examine some of the aspects of self. You are also given the chance to think about how you define *your self*.

In one sense, the self is part of the body. We cannot easily think about a sense of self that is somehow detached from the body. If it was, where would it be? To many, the sense of self seems to be located in the brain. But that does not solve all the problems of self, either. If the brain is the centre of the self, is the rest of the body just 'tacked on'? Clearly not. The self involves all of the body. In this way, it is accurate to say that we *are* our bodies. Our bodies are part of ourselves as much as our brain is a part. Our arm and legs make up our sense of self as much as our 'personality' does. Yet it is surprisingly easy to talk in a way that suggests that our bodies are mere appendages. Think about the following expressions:

I don't like my legs
My arms are too fat
My nose is too big

All of these expressions suggest that the talker is 'disowning' part of his/her body. It is as though the legs, arms and nose are appendages attached to this thing called 'self'. Rather as a motorist may attach various gadgets to her car. This cannot be right. The sense of self contains *everything* about us:

- our bodies
- our thoughts
- our feelings
- our perceptions of ourselves
- our beliefs
- our actions

and so on.

The more we can come to 'own' all aspects of ourselves, the more integrated we become as people. Currently, nursing is taking an increasing interest in 'holism' — the care of the whole person. We as nurses must also take care for the whole of us: our physical, psychological, spiritual and interpersonal aspects. To ignore one or more of these is to ignore something of who we are.

In this first chapter, you are invited to explore various aspects of who you are. The exercises in this chapter come under the following headings:

- The physical aspect of self
- The real self
- The ideal self
- The self-for-others
- The social self
- The spiritual self
- The darker aspect of self
- The sexual self

Work through the exercises in this section slowly and examine what your concept of self is.

	KNOW YOURSELF Questions about this section					
1	The 'self' describes something more than just 'body' and 'mind'	SA	A	U	D	SD
2	It is confusing to talk of the body as being part of the 'self'	SA	A	U	D	SD
3	The 'self' is the whole of a person: everything about them	SA	A	U	D	SD

■ ASPECTS OF THE SELF

The Physical Self

The physical self is your *bodily* sense of self. As was noted above, it is very easy to talk or think of the body as some sort of appendage attached to the self.

Notice, too, that we communicate with others through our physical sense of self. This is sometimes referred to as *body language*. The main elements of non-verbal communication or body language are:

- Eye contact
- Touch
- Gesture
- Proximity to others
- Non-verbal aspects of speech: tone of voice, volume, etc.,
- Facial expression

One way that we can monitor our body language is to pay attention to it. It is probably a myth that other people can read our body language 'like a book' but it is true that the way we present ourselves physically does convey messages to other people. Consider how you are sitting or standing now. Do you hunch your shoulders? Are you frowning? Are the relaxed? Now consider what you are like when you are talking to other people. Do you sit or stand easily and comfortably? Do you make a reasonable amount of eye contact when you are talking to other people? Do you stand close to other people or do you like to keep your distance? All of these factors help to convey to others something of who we are. Gerard Egan [2] suggests that when we engage in a therapeutic conversation with other people, that conversation is enhanced if we pay attention to the following behaviours:

- Sit or stand *squarely* in relation to other people. If we want people to see us as caring and interested, we need to face them as we listen to them.
- Sit in an *open* position. That is to say, try not to sit with crossed arms. Consider, also, not sitting with your legs crossed (although, in this culture, most people seem to cross their legs when sitting down). A 'closed' position, with arms and legs crossed, can convey a sense of defensiveness to the other person.
- Lean slightly towards the person that you are listening to. Again, if we want to show interest, we need to demonstrate that interest.
- Make comfortable eye contact with the other person. Eye contact is influenced by a number of factors: our level of comfortableness with the other person, how much we like them, whether or not we are embarrassed, and so on. If we want to convey interest in the other person, we must be prepared to look at them as they talk and as we listen.

- Relax. When we are with another person in therapeutic conversation with them, we do not need to rehearse what we are going to say to them. Nor do we have to think about what we will be doing next. All we have to do is sit and give our attention to them. If the other person is going to talk easily to us, it is important that we relax.

Read through these suggested behaviours and note any that you have trouble with. Does your non-verbal behaviour encourage or discourage people? What can you do about *changing* your body language? As we have noted, one way is to slowly become *conscious* of it and pay attention to it. In this way, we learn to make what Heron [3] and Peplau [4] call 'conscious use of self'. Rather than just letting our body language happen, we exercise some conscious control over it. If any of our behaviour is to change, we must first be aware of what that behaviour consists of.

This is not to say that we should suddenly become self-conscious and awkward. This sort of thing takes time. It helps if we can begin to notice a little of our behaviour at a time. One way to start is to notice how you sit in relation to your client or patient. As you notice this, decide on what you need to do to enhance the likelihood of your demonstrating a caring attitude towards that person. In doing this, you may choose to slightly modify your body language.

In the first exercise, you are invited to explore how you feel about your own physical sense of self.

EXERCISE	**Number 1**
Aim of exercise:	To explore your physical sense of self
Activity:	Take a sheet of lined paper. Divide it into three columns. Head the first column with the name of someone you like. Head the second column with the name of someone you dislike. Head the third column with your own name. (If you are doing this exercise with other people, it may be more tactful to use codes for the first two columns!).

Under the first column, jot down a description of the physical attributes of the person that you like. Do this in as much detail as you can. Try to describe as many physical features as you can.

Then repeat the activity with the second column. Jot down a description of the physical attributes of the person that you dislike. Again, try to include as much detail as you can.

Finally, write a description of your own physical attributes. Then read through the three descriptions and ask yourself the following questions:

- In what ways are all three descriptions similar?
- In what ways are they different?
- Who got described in greatest detail?

- What is it about your friend's physical appearance that you most like?
- What is it about your friend's appearance that you least like?
- What do you most and least like about the appearance of the person that you do not like?
- Which of those two people are YOU most similar too in appearance?
- In what ways would you like to be physically different?

Variations: 1   Consider the following activity. In what ways are two of the three people in your description similar and yet different to the third person? Try the following pairs of people and ask that question:

- You and the person you like
- You and the person you dislike
- The person you like and the person you dislike
- You and another person that is not on your sheet
- You and one of your parents
- You and a lecturer in the college of nursing

This is a variation on the activity described by George Kelly in his work on Personal Construct Theory [5].

2   Write a description of your physical appearance from the points of view of the person you like and the person you dislike. To what extent do you feel that the descriptions are accurate?

KNOW YOURSELF   Questions about this section

1	I am generally happy with the way I look	SA	A	U	D	SD
2	Physical appearance is not particularly important	SA	A	U	D	SD
3	Too much emphasis is placed on the way nurses 'look'	SA	A	U	D	SD

The Real Self

The real self is that part of you that is most 'internal'. It is the part that you know very well but that probably only a few other people know very well. We often invest quite a lot of energy in keeping this part of ourselves hidden. Often we fear that if other people get to know the 'real me', they may not like us. Oddly, though, it is often the case that what *we* hide from others exactly matches what *other people* hide from us. Carl

Rogers [6] alluded to this when he wrote that 'what is most personal is most general'. He found that what I hide from others is often what they hide from me.

It is interesting that in nursing we often ask patients to disclose a considerable amount of their real selves to us. We often expect that they will talk about quite personal things in the course of being cared for. Yet when the boot is on the other foot and we are asked to disclose who we are, we often feel quite nervous. It is interesting to reflect on why this should be so and also on if it is reasonable to expect patients to talk about themselves readily when we are less able to do so. Sidney Jourard [7] suggested that 'disclosure begets disclosure'. The process of telling others about ourselves is often part of the process of helping them to tell us who they are.

Perhaps if we are to develop greater therapeutic skills as nurses we must be prepared to share who we are with other people. In one sense, we do this all the time. We talk to our friends and our family about who we are. On the other hand, it is quite easy to go through other aspects of life with others knowing very little about us. Consider, for instance, the people you work with. How well do they know you? Think about the lecturers in your college of nursing: do they know you as a person or do they mostly only know you as a student? If so, why is this the case?

It is not being suggested that we should go around pouring ourselves out to everyone we meet, only that if we want to help others as nurses, we must be prepared to let other people get to know us better. That process involves self-disclosure. You cannot get to know another person if they are not prepared to tell you who they are!

On the other hand, there is an argument which suggests that we do not have a 'real self' but that we play out many different roles in our life, according to the circumstances we find ourself in. As Shakespeare put it:

> All the world's a stage,
> And all the men and women merely players,
> They have their exits and their entrances;
> And one man in his time plays out many parts.

In this approach to the self, the self is composed of various roles and performances that we play out. When I am lecturing, for example, I am playing out my 'teacher' role. When I am at home, I am in the 'husband' and 'father' role (and sometimes in the 'ogre' role!). These in turn are different to the role I play as a 'friend' when I go to the pub with someone I know well. This approach to understanding the self has been called the dramaturgical approach and is summed up by Schlenker [8] like this:

> There are numerous similarities between our daily lives and the theater. We possess scripts that allow us to know what to expect in situations. We select words, gestures, and props to illustrate our character just as an author does in fleshing out the characters in a play. There is a front stage where we're 'on' to our associates.

Perhaps you will prefer viewing the 'real self' as a collection of scripts and roles that we acquire over the years of our life rather in the way that an actor learns a wide variety of sets of lines.

EXERCISE	**Number 2**
Aim of exercise:	To explore your real self
Activity:	Take a few sheets of lined paper. Write a description of yourself in the 'third person'. Thus, begin the piece as follows:
	'Jane Smith is a student nurse who . . .'
	Write as quickly as possible and try not to edit what you write. Write as much as you can and in as much detail as you can. If you are doing this exercise on your own, try to write down *everything* that comes to mind. If you are doing it with another person or with a group, notice what comes to mind but that you avoid committing to paper. What would happen if other people knew about the things you are not writing down?
Variations:	Alternatively (or as well as), try writing a lengthy piece about yourself *as you*. Thus, start the piece:
	'I am a student nurse who . . .'

KNOW YOURSELF   Questions about this section

1	I would like more people to know me as I really am	SA	A	U	D	SD
2	Letting other people know too much about you is a dangerous thing	SA	A	U	D	SD
3	I enjoy letting other people know more about me	SA	A	U	D	SD

The Ideal Self

Most of us day dream about how we would like to be. We look at other people and compare ourselves to them. Usually such comparisons are overlaid with fantasies about what a good life the other person leads. We have, then, a picture in our heads of our ideal self.

EXERCISE	**Number 3**
Aim of exercise:	To explore how you would LIKE to be
Activity:	On a sheet of paper, jot down the names of three people that you admire. Now write down what it is that you admire about them. Compare that list with the way that you see yourself. To what degree do you aspire to the characteristics of those people? How like them are you already? What do you *not* admire about those people? If you identify very specific things about one or more of the people on your list that you would like to aspire to yourself, ask yourself: 'what do I need to do to achieve this?' Identify the degree to which *you* could be like the people that you admire.
Variations:	Write out a description of the person that *you would like to be.* How different is this description from how you are already? What do you need to do to become this sort of person? Would you be happier being like this? What would be the drawbacks of being this 'ideal' person? You may find through doing this exercise that you are happier and more successful being yourself!

KNOW YOURSELF   Questions about this section

1	My 'ideal self' is very different to who I am at present	SA	A	U	D	SD
2	It is better to be *me* than to want to be like someone else	SA	A	U	D	SD
3	You cannot change the way you are	SA	A	U	D	SD

The Self for Others

So far, we have concentrated on what it feels like to be 'me' from the inside: the internal or personal sense of self. Allied to this is the self that we present to other people. Who we are when we are with others depends on a number of factors: our relationship with the other person, whether or not we like or love them, whether or not we feel secure with them, whether or not they are of higher status in the organisation than we are.

One important aspect of this self-for-others is that other people often have a different view of us than the view we have of ourselves. More than this, they often act *as though that view was the accurate one.* People treat us as though we are the person they imagine us to be. Also, they try to shape who we are by letting us know the degree to which we conform, or otherwise, that view. In this sense, other people are telling us who we are. Consider parents, for example. They frequently tell children that they should 'not behave like that' or ask them 'not to be like that'. In this way, they mould and shape their children (or try to!) towards their own view of how those children should be.

This process continues with friends, colleagues, teachers and patients or clients. All of them have a view of us and all of them want us, to a greater or lesser extent, to conform to that view. If we do not, they frequently complain or exert pressure on us to change. The big question, here, is: to what degree do we comply with the needs and wishes of others? To what degree do we allow ourselves to be moulded in this way?

EXERCISE	**Number 4**
Aim of exercise:	To explore your presentation of self with other people
Activity:	Write down the names of the following people:

- A teacher that you like or admire
- A teacher that you dislike
- A close friend
- One of your parents

Now imagine yourself with each one of these people in turn. Write a short description of how you present yourself to each of them. Consider, for example:

- Whether or not you are relaxed with them
- Whether or not you can talk to them easily
- Whether or not you disclose much about yourself to them
- Whether or not you feel embarrassed when you are with them
- How you feel when you are in their company, and so on

Now work through those descriptions and note the degrees to which you are *the same* with all of those people and the degrees to which you are *different* with them. All of these features are elements of your self-for-others. Most of us are multi-faceted and change our way of relating to people according to who those people are and the relationship we have with them.

1	I am always the same with people, no matter who they are	SA	A	U	D	SD
2	It is important to be yourself; if people do not like me as I am, that is their hard luck	SA	A	U	D	SD
3	There are some people with whom I find it very difficult to be myself	SA	A	U	D	SD

The Social Self

Apart from the way others see us, there is also the question of how we present ourselves in groups. Consider, for example, the difference between 'you' in a learning group in the college of nursing and 'you' in a pub or cafe with a group of friends. What relation does the 'you' in the classroom bear to the 'you' in the social situation? Do you recognise the two? Which do you prefer?

As we noted above, many people bring pressure to bear on us to become the way that *they* think we should be. On a somewhat larger scale, the process of *socialisation* is also at work to ensure that we act in a certain way. Socialisation is the process by which we become introduced to and learn the particular values of a society or a situation. In nursing, occupational socialisation is at work. The process of becoming a nurse involves, to a greater or lesser degree, the process of absorbing and integrating the values and beliefs that go with being a nurse. Almost without noticing it, we are being encouraged to 'act like a nurse'. Some of this influence comes from the college of nursing where nurses are taught what nursing is about in a rather formal way. Socialisation is perhaps at its strongest, though, in the clinical setting. We learn a lot about being a nurse through being with other nurses. The question, here, is: to what degree do we give up our own individuality in order to take on board the values and actions required of us as professionals?

Our personalities also affect the degree to which we feel comfortable with groups of people. Some people, either naturally or through socialisation, are more extrovert and outgoing than others. In the following exercise, you are encouraged to reflect on how you mix with others. If we can identify the particular sorts of situations that we find difficult or awkward, we are in a better position to change or modify ourselves. There is, of course, no obligation to change. The only reasons for changing how we are when working or mixing with groups are: (a) because we are not comfortable or (b) other people require us to mix or work in groups.

EXERCISE	**Number 5**
Aim of exercise:	To explore the social aspect of self

Activity:	Consider the following social situations and write notes on how you both *feel* and *behave* in them:

- A large party at a friend's house where there are a lot of people that you do not know
- A case conference or ward meeting
- A learning group in the college of nursing
- A wedding
- A prize giving or other formal situation

Now ask yourself the following questions:

- In which of these situations are you the most comfortable?
- What do you *do* when you feel uncomfortable in the presence of others?
- How do you react to other people who are more shy than you?
- How do you react to people who are more extrovert than you?
- Do you want to be different? If so, in what ways?

KNOW YOURSELF   Questions about this section

1	I prefer mixing with small groups of people rather than large groups	SA	A	U	D	SD
2	People are people; I am quite happy in any social situation	SA	A	U	D	SD
3	I think that it is important to pay attention to how I present myself to other people in groups	SA	A	U	D	SD

The Spiritual Self

A particularly personal aspect of self is the spiritual one. Whilst the word 'spiritual' is often associated with religion, it need not necessarily be. Another way of thinking about spirituality is to think of it in terms of the need that each of us has for *meaning* in our lives. Bruno Bettelheim noted that people can put up with almost anything if they can see the reason for it [9]. Most of us need a sense of purpose in what we do.

For some, this purpose does come through a religious conviction. For others, that purpose is framed in political, philosophical or psychological terms. In the end, the spiritual sense of self is concerned with what you *believe in*.

Why is it important to be clear about what you believe in? First, it helps us to avoid assuming that everyone else thinks about things the way that we do. If we are unreflective, there is a great tendency for this to happen. We assume that if we think a certain way it is likely that other people do too.

Second, being clear about what we believe in can help us when we are faced with patients or clients who have lost a sense of meaning. We will be more secure in our own sense of self and less likely to 'preach' to them. It is not appropriate, in a professional nursing setting, to try to convince other people that our beliefs or values are the right ones. As Carl Rogers [10] points out, people are better off when they are allowed to draw their own conclusions about their lives and their beliefs. In this sense, no one ever makes another person's mind up for them. We all have to come to our beliefs for ourselves. Whilst others often influence us, in the end it is we who decide what it is that we do and do not believe.

It is sometimes suggested that anything to do with spirituality is far too personal to discuss. If we are concerned with nursing the whole person and with holistic care, then part of that caring is to do with the spiritual aspects of their lives. If we have not considered our own beliefs and values we are less likely to be able to help others to think and talk through theirs.

EXERCISE	**Number 6**
Aim of exercise:	To explore your spiritual beliefs
Activity:	Write a short passage that sums up what you believe in. Use the following questions to help:

- Do you believe in God?
- If you do, what does your concept of God involve?
- Would you call yourself a religious person?
- Would you call yourself an atheist?
- If you are an atheist, what do you think about people who believe in God?
- If you believe in God, what do you think about atheists?
- Do you believe that there is more to life than what we can see, hear, taste, touch or smell?
- If so, what . . . ?
- Do you believe in life after death?
- Do you believe that life has a 'meaning'?
- How did you develop your beliefs?
- Where did your beliefs come from?
  and so on.

Variations:	Try this activity with a friend or with a small group of people. Share your beliefs with this other person or with the group and note the degree to which you agree or disagree with each other.

EXERCISE	**Number 7**
Aim of exercise:	To explore your feelings about other people's beliefs
Activity:	Read through the following statements and decide on how you would respond to each other.

1   A colleague tries to convert you to their particular set of religious beliefs. Would you . . .
(a) Tell them that you have a different point of view
(b) Tell them that you do not want to hear what they have to say
(c) Tell them that religion is a personal thing and that it should not be discussed
(d) Tell them that you do not believe in God
(e) Say something else

2   A friend says that he does not believe in God. Would you . . .
(a) Accept what he says as his point of view
(b) Try to change his way of thinking
(c) Feel a duty to try to persuade him that God exists
(d) Tell him that he will change his mind one day
(e) Say something else

3   An evangelist knocks on your front door. Would you . . .
(a) Ask her to go away
(b) Listen to what she has to say
(c) Say that you have a different religious point of view
(d) Try to argue with her
(e) Get angry with her
(f) Say or do something else

4   A lecturer in the college of nursing begins a discussion on religion and spirituality. Would you . . .
(a) Join in the discussion
(b) Prefer to remain out of the discussion
(c) Become angry with other people's lack of understanding
(d) Suggest that the topic is too personal
(e) Say or do something else

5   A patient asks you to pray with her. Would you . . .
(a) Do so
(b) Become embarrassed

(c) Apologise and say that you're not religious

(d) Suggest that you call a minister

(e) Say or do something else

6 A patient says that he feels that life is meaningless. Would you . . .

(a) Tell him not to be so pessimistic

(b) Tell him about God

(c) Explore his feelings with him

(d) Tell him that you will call a senior nurse to talk to him

(e) Tell him that life has plenty of meaning and that it is wrong to talk that way

(f) Say or do something else

Variations:

Consider your reactions to each of the above situations and explore what it might be like to react in *exactly the opposite* way to the one you have identified. Consider, also, what it might be like to hold *exactly the opposite* views on spirituality to the ones that you hold at present.

EXERCISE	**Number 8**
Aim of exercise:	To explore what you find easy and difficult to accept in the spiritual domain
Activity:	Read through the following statements and note the degree to which you agree, disagree or are uncertain about each of the statements.

1 There is only one true religion.

AGREE   UNCERTAIN   DISAGREE

2 Most religions contain at least a grain of truth.

AGREE   UNCERTAIN   DISAGREE

3 God is a person.

AGREE   UNCERTAIN   DISAGREE

4 God does not exist.

AGREE   UNCERTAIN   DISAGREE

5 There is life after death.

AGREE   UNCERTAIN   DISAGREE

6 There is all there is. When you die, that is the end of you.

AGREE   UNCERTAIN   DISAGREE

7 Religion is important from a cultural point of view.

AGREE   UNCERTAIN   DISAGREE

8   No religion is completely true.

     AGREE   UNCERTAIN   DISAGREE

9   I can see no point in religious activities.

     AGREE   UNCERTAIN   DISAGREE

10   My religious beliefs are one of the most important aspects of my life.

      AGREE   UNCERTAIN   DISAGREE

KNOW YOURSELF	Questions about this section				
1	My spiritual beliefs and values are personal, private issues that should not concern anyone but me	SA	A	U	D	SD
2	I would prefer to skip this section	SA	A	U	D	SD
3	Everyone, in the end, has *some* religious beliefs	SA	A	U	D	SD

The Darker Self

Most of us have a few skeletons in the cupboard – aspects of ourselves that we do not particularly like. Sometimes we invest an awful lot of energy in keeping those aspects of ourselves private. Sometimes, this is appropriate. It would not do to tell everyone about ourselves and what we think and feel. On the other hand, it seems a pity if there are aspects of ourselves that we cannot talk to *anyone* about. Often, the 'darker', hidden aspect of our self is concerned with thoughts about:

- Aggressive feelings towards others
- Certain sexual thoughts and feelings
- Feelings that we think are 'odd'
- Feelings and thoughts that we are sure no one else has

The darker side of the person is dealt with in some detail in the literature of fiction. Jean-Paul Sartre's non-hero in his novel *Nausea* [11] is clearly familiar with it, as is Hesse's character, Harry Haller, in that writer's *Steppenwolf* [12]. It is interesting to read how writers have portrayed this darker side of the person. Clearly, some of the writing is autobiographical. Sartre was later to note that the main character in *Nausea* was based on himself [13].

Sometimes, when the darker side of the person is acknowledged, it makes him or her feel something of an 'outsider' – a person who does not necessarily conform with society and abide by its norms. Perhaps the classic work on this is Colin Wilson's *The*

Outsider: a classic study of alienation and creativity in literature [14]. A radical view might be that nursing could do with a few more 'outsiders'. Perhaps nurses are, as a rule, to ready to conform.

One of the lessons that arise out of psychotherapy is that the thoughts and feelings that most of us hide are the thoughts and feelings that most of us hide! Or, put another way, as Carl Rogers notes: 'What is most personal is most general' [10]. When we *do* share the darker side of ourselves with another person, we often find that not only are we not alone in our thoughts and feelings but that also many other people think and feel as we do. It may be helpful if we share some of those thoughts and feelings with others occasionally. Bottled up, they tend to get out of proportion. Talked about, occasionally, they regain their perspective.

Simone Weil, the 20th century catholic mystic, seems to have been both aware of the darker side of herself and prepared to face it when she wrote:

> I have the germ of all possible crimes, or nearly all, within me . . . The crimes horrified me, but they did not surprise me; I felt the possibility of them within myself; it was actually because I felt this possibility in myself that they filled me with such horror. This natural disposition is dangerous and very painful, but, like every variety of natural disposition, it can be put to good purpose . . . [15]

What do *you* think about your darker side? Ignore it? Pretend it is not there? Or do you feel that, on the whole, it is better to look on the bright side and that concentrating on the darker side can only depress you?

EXERCISE	**Number 9**
Aim of exercise:	To explore the 'darker' aspect of the self
Activity:	This activity does not involve writing anything down. Just make a mental note of *what you would not disclose* about yourself to the following people:

- Colleagues at work
- Relatives other than immediate family
- Members of your family
- Close friends
- Your closest friend
- Your spouse

Note, too, if there are things that you would not disclose about yourself to *anyone*. Now ask yourself WHY you would not disclose things to these various people. What would happen if you did?

KNOW YOURSELF	Questions about this section					
1	There are certain things that I should not tell other people	SA	A	U	D	SD
2	It is important that at least one person knows most of your secrets	SA	A	U	D	SD
3	If people have particularly dark secrets they shouldn't be in nursing	SA	A	U	D	SD

The Sexual Self

We are all sexual beings. Two aspects of sexuality may be described: (a) our sexual identity and (b) our sexual orientation. The former refers to whether or not we are male or female (although it also refers to the degree to which we *feel* male or female). Sexual identity is not just a physical issue: we are socialised into sexual roles from an early age and learn to identify certain behaviours, thoughts and values as 'male' or 'female'.

Our sexual orientation refers to how we prefer to *express* our sexuality. At least three options exist here: heterosexual orientation, where we choose to express our sexuality towards people of the opposite sex; homosexual, where we choose to express our sexuality towards people of the same sex; bisexual, where we choose to express our sexuality towards people of both sexes.

Clearly, in our society, heterosexuality has tended to be the statistical norm for sexual orientation. This has led to those who have a homosexual orientation being treated with varying degrees of stigma. Those with a bisexual orientation barely get a mention at all and seem not to fit easily into either group. The fact of heterosexuality being the norm has tended to mean that those with a homosexual or bisexual orientation often experience considerable guilt about the way they feel. How do you feel about YOUR sexual orientation? How did you develop it? How do you feel about the notion of 'choosing' your orientation?

Amanda Gunner, in a paper about sexual prejudice in nursing [16], suggests that there are at least four factors involved in exploring your sexual relationships:

- Your own attitude towards sex
- Your perception of your own child as a sexual being
- Your own concept of sex education
- Your own use of language when discussing sexual matters

Gunner's four points may be a useful starting point for exploring the background to *your* sexuality and may be transposed thus:

- What is your attitude towards sex: positive or negative?

- What acknowledgement did your parents make of your sexuality when you were a child?
- What sort of sex education did you have?
- What words do you use when discussing sexual matters?

EXERCISE	**Number 10**
Aim of exercise:	To explore aspects of your sexual identity and orientation
Activity:	Jot down on a sheet of paper the headings MALE and FEMALE. Under each heading jot down words that you associate with each. When you have done that consider the degree to which YOU fulfil the male or female criteria that you have generated. Then, consider your own sexual orientation. What do you consider yourself: heterosexual, homosexual or bisexual? Do you fit neatly into one of these categories? Can you imagine yourself *changing* your sexual orientation? How do you feel about people whose orientation is different to your own? Why?
Variations:	If you can, it is useful to do this activity with a group of colleagues or friends. Try to accept each others differences of opinion.

KNOW YOURSELF   Questions about this section

1	Most people would prefer to be heterosexual, given the choice	SA	A	U	D	SD
2	Homosexuals are born homosexual	SA	A	U	D	SD
3	I could not imagine changing my sexual orientation	SA	A	U	D	SD

■ PUTTING IT ALL TOGETHER

These are some aspects of what makes up the self. Review this chapter and think about which parts of it you found the most difficult to work through. Which are the aspects of YOU that you find most thought provoking or problematic? Do you feel that you should work more on these areas or do you feel that some aspects of your self are particularly personal — too personal to share with others?

■ SUMMARY OF THIS CHAPTER

This chapter has begun the exploration of self. It has identified the following aspects of self:

- The physical aspect of self
- The real self
- The ideal self
- The self-for-others
- The social self
- The spiritual self
- The darker aspect of self
- The sexual self

2 | Self-awareness

The folly of that impossible precept, 'Know thyself';
till it be translated into this partially possible one,
'Know what thou canst work at'.

THOMAS CARLYLE

A person learns significantly only those things which
he perceives as being involved in the maintenance of,
or enhancement of, the structure of self.

CARL ROGERS

Keywords	● Self-awareness
	● Models of self
	● Mental defence mechanisms
	● The Johari Window
	● Self-awareness methods

Aims of this	● To explore the concept of self-awareness
chapter	● To examine ways of becoming more self-aware
	● To relate self-awareness to nursing
	● To explore some problems in trying to become self-aware

■ WHAT IS SELF-AWARENESS?

In the first chapter, the notion of the self was discussed. In this chapter we consider what self-awareness is and why it is useful to have it. In its simplest sense, self awareness is the continuous and evolving process of getting to know who you are. It is coming to know more about those aspects of self discussed in the first chapter. There is, however, another way of thinking about self-awareness.

First, it is necessary to acknowledge that there are at least two broad aspects to each of us: the inner experience and the outer experience (Fig. 2.1). The inner experience is how we feel inside. In the diagram the inner experience has been further divided up into five aspects: thinking, feeling, sensing, intuiting and the sense of the body.

The outer experience is that aspect of us that other people see: our verbal and non-verbal behaviour and the way we look and dress. The rest of this book is taken up with exploring this inner and outer sense of self. In a way, the outer experience is all that others see of us. We must express our inner selves through this outer sense of

OUTER ASPECTS OF SELF   INNER ASPECT OF SELF

Eye contact Facial expression Gestures	THINKING	FEELING
Touch Proximity to others Movement	SENSING	INTUITING
Dress Paralinguistics etc.	EXPERIENCE OF THE BODY	

Figure 2.1. A model of the inner and outer aspects of self.

self. No one else sees what goes on 'inside'. On the other hand, the outer sense of self is very much affected by the inner. We cannot think or feel without its being expressed through our outer, bodily sense of self. We are constantly communicating to others, this inner self. The vehicle of that expression is our body.

■ **OUTER ASPECTS OF SELF**

It is worth considering the outer aspect of the above model a little more closely. What do others see of us? First, they see our physical presence – what we look like. Then, in a more specific sense they understand what we say to them through our non-verbal communication (NVC). This comprises eye contact, facial expression, gesture, touch and proximity to others. It is interesting to reflect on what affects our using non verbal communication. Consider, for instance:

- In what circumstances you find eye contact with another person difficult?
- To what degree you consider that you have an 'expressive' face?
- What sort of hand and arm gestures you use when talking?
- To what degree you allow or expect other people to touch you when they are talking to you?
- How close or how distant you like to stand in relation to another person?

Many of these things will be dependent upon (a) our relationship with the other person in terms of whether we are junior or senior in rank to them and (b) our feelings about them. Consider, now, the issues of eye contact, facial expression, gesture, touch and proximity in relation to the following people in your life:

- One of your parents
- Your boy or girl friend (or husband or wife)
- An elderly patient
- A patient your own age
- Your best friend
- A relative stranger of the same sex
- A relative stranger of the opposite sex

It is likely that with each of these people you use different sorts of non-verbal communication. As you come to notice how you express yourself with various people via the use of body language, notice, too, what sort of non-verbal communication is *effective* and what is less so. For example, what we say to other people is usually received best if we are able to make eye contact with them. On the other hand, it is easy to overestimate the amount of touch that other people will allow. Some people are 'high touchers' and some are low. Whilst nursing is a 'hands on' profession, we cannot assume that everyone is happy to be touched.

Finally, in this discussion of non-verbal behaviour, consider that element of communication that is not strictly non-verbal: paralinguistics. The term is used to cover all of those aspects of speech that are not speech themselves: tone of voice, volume, timing, use of 'um's and err's', accent and so forth. Try to become aware of how you use your voice in this way and how others use theirs. Consider, for example, the different ways that paralinguistics are used in the following situations:

- By a teacher giving a lecture
- By a nurse who is comforting a bereaved person
- By a doctor talking to a patient on a ward round
- By a senior nurse talking to a junior nurse
- By friends talking together
- By members of a family

Again, like non-verbal communication, it is possible to notice a wide range of different uses of paralinguistic aspects of speech. It is also possible to consciously use your voice in order to convey various things about you. It is important that your tone of voice matches what you have to say. It is no use, for example, trying to tell someone that you are angry by using a gentle, quiet tone of voice. The ability to match *what you say* with the appropriate *non-verbal behaviour* and the *correct use of paralinguistics* is known as *congruence*. The congruent communicator is one who says what she means, uses the appropriate eye contact and gestures and who is able to modulate her voice to match both of those two elements. Consider your own levels of congruence in the following situations:

- When you want to tell someone that you are angry with them
- When you are in a shop complaining about an aspect of service

- When you are trying to tell someone that you are very fond of them
- When you are breaking bad news to someone in a hospital setting
- When you are talking to a member of your family

■ INNER ASPECTS OF SELF

These are elements of the external aspect of self. In turning to the internal elements we consider Jung's four functions of the mind: thinking, feeling, sensing and intuiting [17]. These are the components that go to make up what goes on inside our heads.

The notion of thinking is fairly self-explanatory: it is what we do when we puzzle to try to work things out. The 'feeling' aspect of the mind is concerned with the emotions. The 'sensing' aspect is that part that interprets what comes in through the senses – what we see, taste, touch, smell or hear. The intuitive aspect is the part of us that depends upon 'hunches' or 'knowledge beyond the senses'. Sometimes we seem to 'know' things for which we have no evidence. As Michael Polanyi [18], the philosopher of science noted: 'we know more than we can tell'.

Allied to these psychological aspects is the fact that we have an inner experience of the body. In one sense, this manifests itself through actual visceral feelings: we are able to sense pain or discomfort, relaxation or tension. In another sense it is also about how we *feel* about our bodies: the sense we have of whether or not we are underweight, overweight, attractive, unattractive and so on. Notice that these personal estimations of how we look may have little to do with how others perceive us. It is as though we build up our own internal picture of the way we look. Sometimes this is developed out of what others tell us. Sometimes it is linked to our sense of self-worth and confidence. Usually if we *feel* good about ourselves we think that we *look* reasonable. If, on the other hand, we lack confidence or are depressed, we experience our sense of the body as negative. How do you feel about *your* body?

The four aspects of mind described by Jung are the subject matter of the next four chapters of this book. Briefly, Jung noted that although our minds dealt with thinking, feeling, sensing and intuiting, we tended not to be well developed in all four of those aspects. Particularly, he noted that some people developed a thinking/sensing orientation whilst others developed a feeling/intuiting orientation to the world. Thus the person who was basically a thinking/sensing person tended to see things logically and want explanations for things. The feeling/intuiting type, on the other hand, tended to rely on emotional feelings and 'hunches'.

Note the degree to which YOU fall into either one of these two groupings. Do you rely heavily on logic and explanation? Do you tend to take the attitude 'I'll believe it when I see it'? Or do you tend to be led a lot by your feelings and believe that you 'shouldn't analyse things too much'? Either way, you may be missing out on another possible aspect of your self! You can, after all, be logical *and* emotional, depending on the circumstance.

KNOW YOURSELF   Questions about this section

1	I am generally fairly happy with the way I look	SA	A	U	D	SD
2	I see myself as more logical than emotional	SA	A	U	D	SD
3	I often compare the way I look and talk with the way other people look and talk	SA	A	U	D	SD

■ WHY IS SELF-AWARENESS NECESSARY?

This book is about self-awareness and about getting to know yourself better. Why do nurses need to know themselves? At least six reasons can be identified:

1   To enhance self-understanding
2   To allow acceptance of others
3   To enable us to handle difficult situations
4   To increase conscious use of the self
5   To enable self-monitoring
6   To enhance personal autonomy

First, the process of developing self-awareness allows us to get to know how we think and feel. It allows us to clarify our values and beliefs and gets us to think about our experience of the world. Without some sort of self understanding we will find it difficult to understand other people.

As we get to know ourselves better we also get a better understanding of our strengths and deficits. This can allow us to prepare for difficult situations. For example, if you know that you are distressed by people who cry and have some understanding of your own emotional make up, you are better placed to help the person who *does* cry – even if that means finding someone else to help. If you do not know your limitations, you are more likely to discover them when faced with a difficult situation or relationship. In this sense, to be forewarned is to be forearmed.

Part of the process of developing self-awareness is the allied process of achieving conscious use of the self. We have at least two choices. We can live life without any awareness of how we appear to others. We can just allow ourselves to 'happen'. Alternatively, we can notice what we do and say and consciously use our verbal and non-verbal behaviour in therapeutic ways. Initially, this can involve a bit of acting. Just as an actor has to learn lines and practice moves, so too does the person who is learning conscious use of self have to try out new phrases and behaviours. This does not have to mean that we become 'unnatural' and stilted in the way that we relate to others. It is just to note that if we want to become more helpful and therapeutic in our dealings with others we have to be prepared to *change* a little. We cannot change ourselves until we know ourselves. Thus, self-awareness is the first stage in learning how to use ourselves as therapeutic agents.

Allied to this conscious use of self is the notion of self-monitoring. We are in a far better position to take care of ourselves if we notice how we react in various situations. Thus, if we know beforehand that we tend to be stressed by exams or by other people's emotion, we can learn to take action to cope with these situations. Also, we can learn to read our own signs of stress or discomfort and take action before we become too stressed or upset. One of the reasons that people burn out in the caring professions is that they do not notice that they are under pressure until it is too late. One of the most important aspects of becoming self-aware is the ability to notice what is happening to you and take the appropriate action.

Perhaps most important of all, self-awareness can give us more freedom. If we do not notice what happens to us, how we react, what we think and feel and so on, we are limited in what we can decide for ourselves. The process of getting to know ourselves better is also the process of coming to identify our life options. As we become more self-aware we can become less acted upon and more of an agent – a person who chooses and decides for herself. The next series of exercises explores these aspects of the need for self awareness.

EXERCISE	**Number 11**
Aim of exercise:	To explore ways of increasing self-understanding
Activity:	Divide a sheet of paper up under the following headings:

- Thinking
- Feeling
- Sensing
- Intuiting

Now write brief notes under each heading about ways that you might increase your awareness of these aspects of yourself. If you are working with a partner or a small group it will be helpful if you discuss your findings. Consider, at least, the following approaches to developing self-understanding:

- Through self-disclosure
- Through reports from other people
- Through exercise and activity
- Through diaries or journals

EXERCISE	**Number 12**
Aim of exercise:	To explore acceptance of others
Activity:	Write out a list of the sorts of people you do not like. Note any particular characteristics that those people have, any mannerisms, attitudes and so on. Then read through your list and consider the degree to which *you* have any of those mannerisms, attitudes and so forth. Consider, also, what aspects of yourself you do not readily accept. Then ask yourself what would happen if you *did* accept them.

EXERCISE	**Number 13**
Aim of exercise:	To examine nursing situations which you find difficult
Activity:	Read through the following list of situations and put them in order of which you would find most difficult to handle.

- A child on a paediatric ward wants to go home and will not stop crying
- A confused, young patient shouts at you and threatens to hit you
- An elderly man begins to wander off the ward and refuses to come back with you
- A young girl asks your advice about contraception
- A young boy wants to know about AIDS
- A person older than yourself begins to tell you very personal things about herself

Now read through this list and jot down:

1 How each situation would make you feel
2 How you would handle each situation
3 How you feel an *expert* might handle the situation

EXERCISE	**Number 14**
Aim of exercise:	To increase 'conscious use of the self'
Activity:	In some respects, conscious use of the self, or learning to stay aware of what you are doing, is easy. All you have to do is to remember to do it! All that is required in this exercise is to stop reading this book for a while and to notice everything that you do, think and feel for about 5 minutes. It helps

if you pay attention, first, to your behaviour. How, for instance, are you sitting at the moment? How is your breathing: is it deep or shallow? What about your facial expression? Are you smiling, frowning . . . and so on.

When you first do this exercise you are likely to feel fairly self-conscious. This will pass as you become more effective at noticing what you do. Once you have carried out this activity for 5 minutes, stop it and reflect on the experience. This ability to 'notice' yourself is the first major stage in developing self-awareness and the first step towards developing conscious use of the self – the ability to use yourelf as a therapeutic instrument in nursing.

Variations:	Once you have tried this exercise once, decide on a time, at work, when you will notice what you do, think and feel for a period of between 5 and 10 minutes. Then try to carry out the activity at regular intervals. Gradually, you will come to be much more aware of what you say, do, think and feel. Notice, particularly, how you treat other people and how your behaviour changes with different sorts of people – colleagues, patients, friends and so on.

EXERCISE	**Number 15**
Aim of exercise:	To explore aspects of yourself over one day
Activity:	This is a lengthier exercise than the previous one. Find or buy an exercise book. Rule it up so that you have a section of each hour of one day. Then choose a particular day in which to keep the journal. On that day, take detailed notes of everything that you do, feel and think during each hour. You may want to stop each hour and fill in the diary. Alternatively, you may want to make irregular stops to fill it in. Either way, try to account for the whole day in this way. Notice any resistance that you have to writing things down or to completing the journal. At the end of the day, read through the journal and note particular trends, changes or themes that recur.
Variations:	You may want to try this activity on a regular basis. Choose different sorts of day: a day at work, a day at home, a day on holiday. Do you change considerably, depending on where you are and who you are with or are you fairly consistent?

1	I think that I am 'myself' in most situations	SA	A	U	D	SD
2	I find it much easier to be myself with people I know well	SA	A	U	D	SD
3	I am not sure that I could easily be myself with patients at work	SA	A	U	D	SD

■ EXAMPLES OF ITS VALUE IN NURSING

In the discussion above, we considered reasons for becoming self-aware. The point, here, is to develop the theme of self-awareness in nursing. The following exercise asks you to consider people that you know in nursing whom you consider to be self-aware.

EXERCISE	**Number 16**
Aim of exercise:	To explore self-awareness in nursing
Activity:	Divide a sheet of paper with a line down the centre. On the right hand side, write down the names of at least four people from nursing that you consider to be self-aware. In the left hand column, write notes about each person as follows:
	1 What suggests to you that they are self-aware
	2 The advantages that you feel arise out of their being self-aware
	Next, you may want to consider in what ways you are similar to these people and in what ways you are dissimilar. It is quite likely that you will have chosen people that you *like*. Note, as you read through your notes, the things that you do not like about them. This method of comparing positives and negatives is another route to developing self-awareness.
Variations:	You may want to think of people outside of nursing that you consider to have a degree of self-awareness. When you have identified them, note the features that suggest that they do have self-awareness and consider how that awareness helps them in whatever it is that they do. Notice, too, whether or not self-awareness can be a hindrance.

Self-awareness comes into most aspects of nursing. The following is a list of some of the ways it can help you in delivering a high standard of care. Self-awareness is important in:

- Ensuring that people *feel* cared for
- Understanding other people's needs and wants
- Helping people express their feelings
- Coping with other people's pain
- Helping people who are dying
- Helping the bereaved
- Working with children
- Learning nursing
- Doing research
- Understanding your colleagues
- Learning to relax
- Getting on better with your friends and family
- Planning your work
- Identifying your strengths and deficits
- Planning your future
- Identifying your learning needs
- Organising the work of others

	KNOW YOURSELF Questions about this section					
1	Most people I know in nursing are fairly self-aware	SA	A	U	D	SD
2	Most people that I know could benefit by becoming more self-aware	SA	A	U	D	SD
3	I do not like comparing myself to others	SA	A	U	D	SD

▌ HOW WE FOOL OURSELVES

It is not just a case of studying yourself and becoming self-aware. Part of us is too clever for that. This chapter discusses some of the ways in which we fool ourselves by the use of mental defence mechanisms. The notion of defence mechanisms was developed within the psychodynamic school of psychology, beginning with Sigmund Freud [19, 20].

There is some debate in the literature as to whether or not we can be aware of using mental mechanisms. It has been suggested that they happen at an *unconscious* level and that because of that we cannot know that we are using them. Read through the descriptions of them and decide for yourself. Probably it is the case that sometimes we do and sometimes we do not know that we are using them.

Also, the idea of mental mechanisms is not a 'fact': there is no research to show that we definitely do use them. They are best treated as one way of exploring the way we avoid facing certain things about ourselves. Often, too, they help us to understand other people. Treat them as possibilities.

Rationalisation

We can not take too much reality. If the truth becomes too painful we deal with it by giving ourselves a palatable explanation for what is happening. Consider, for example, the person who finds that she has failed her exams and who knows that she has not worked for them. To cope with the disappointment, rather than face her own lack of application, she says:

or
> 'No one could pass an exam like *that*!'
>
> 'That just shows how useless our training really was!'

This is rationalisation. That is not to say that when we offer explanations for what happens to us we are *always* rationalising. The test is if, at a later date, the 'truth' dawns on us in place of our excuses.

Often, rationalisation can help to soften the blow. When something particularly painful happens, like a relationship breaks up, it is helpful to think:

> 'I didn't like him much anyway . . .'

On the other hand, if we are *always* rationalising rather than facing the truth, it suggests we need to look at ourselves a bit closer to see why we need to fool ourselves in this way.

Projection

Another way of dealing with our problems is to see them reflected in other people. Consider the following expressions:

> 'She's alright but she does like the sound of her own voice!'
> 'He's pleasant enough but I don't trust him!'
> 'She's very conceited . . .'

Often what we say about other people says a lot about us. Often, rather than face ourselves, we see our own qualities in other people whilst remaining unaware of those qualities in ourselves. It is rather like the mother watching her son's boy scout parade and who says:

> 'Isn't it odd how they are all out of step except for Simon!'

Rather than see our negative qualities we see other people parading them around in front of us and wonder why other people do not notice all these bad qualities that are so obvious.

Rather like rationalisation, projection can help to soften the blow sometimes. Again, though, if we find that we are always being critical of others and yet remain highly uncritical of ourselves, it is time to rethink a little.

Reaction Formation

This is a particularly curious way of dealing with our problems. Rather than face the way we feel, we express the *opposite*. Thus we hear ourselves say things like:

> 'I'm alright – I'm really cheerful!'
> 'I'm not upset at all: far from it!'
> 'No, I don't like him – he's the last person I would want to go out with.'

It seems that sometimes the only way of coping with how we feel is to play the opposite. One way of checking whether or not reaction formation is occurring is to try *reversing* some of the statements that you make that ring a bit hollow. You may want to try saying (silently!):

> 'I *do* like him – he's the person I really want to go out with.'

Sometimes it works, sometimes it doesn't. Again, it is not the case that every time you make a strong statement that you mean the opposite but sometimes it is worth trying.

Suppression

Another way of avoiding reality is to pretend that it is not there. This is rather like our tucking a telephone bill behind a pile of books and pretending that it has not arrived. When we suppress things, we know that they are there but we choose not to deal with them. Thus we have a nagging feeling that we should be facing the way that we feel about someone but instead we put it off. This is fine as a short term measure and it can give us some breathing space to make decisions. In the long term, though, like the telephone bill, things have to be faced.

Repression

This is a more severe form of suppression. Here, when something traumatic has happened to us, we find that we have no memory of it at all: we have completely sealed off our feelings. Freud argued that children often did this with strong feelings that they had for their parents. As adults, they were unaware that they had such strong feelings but those feelings affected their behaviour, their feelings, their attitudes as adults.

Often, this shows itself in parents 'replaying' the sort of behaviour that *their* parents displayed but without realising it.

According to the psychoanalytical school of psychology, repression is reponsible for all sorts of problems in adult life from difficulties with hidden anger to buried sexual feelings. One of the tasks of psychoanalysis is to make the *unconscious*, conscious. In other words, it aims to help a person face up to the repressed side of themselves. It is true to say, however, that other psychologists question that repression takes place at all and would argue that we have *learned* to act and feel in certain ways. For them, the notion of repression is a non-starter.

Intellectualisation

This is a common one in teachers in colleges and universities! It involves the person finding it necessary to *always* find a rational argument for what is happening. Feelings are unacceptable: rationality is the only thing that is allowed. The person who intellectualises excessively always uses his head rather than his emotions. Mr Spock, in *Star Trek*, was the extreme example of the person who uses intellectualisation. Sometimes we hide behind our thinking: it is somehow safer to think than to feel:

> 'I'm not upset, it's just that I'm having difficulty to coping with this set of contingencies . . .'
> 'I'm prone to using rather a lot of mental defence mechanisms. At the moment, I'm having difficulties rationalising my feelings . . . (!)'

Regression

Sometimes our feelings get too much for us and we return to the safety of rather more infantile behaviour. This is regression. It is when we return to the comfort of an earlier style of behaving rather than acting as mature adults. It is notable that we do this whenever we are threatened. You might, for instance, notice that you regress in your behaviour when you are threatened by a change in your life. You may also regress when you are faced with illness. Unfortunately, nursing and medicine *encourage* people to regress. Quite often, in hospital, we make people put on night attire and put them to bed, thus helping to ensure that they return to a 'cared for' and dependent state reminiscent of childhood. Examples of regression in everyday life include finding ourselves saying things like:

> 'It's not *fair* . . .'
> 'She *always* does better than me . . .'
> 'This bloody car – I don't know why I bother with it!'

These are just some of the ways in which we fool ourselves into thinking that things are other than they are. There are many more. You may want to explore your own defence and look for patterns of ways that you fool yourself.

EXERCISE	**Number 17**
Aim of exercise:	To explore your defence mechanisms
Activity:	Simply notice yourself a little more closely in everyday life. Pay particular attention to how you deal with disappoint-ments and problems in relationships. Try to decide whether or not you feel the notion of mental mechanisms is a valid one for you.
	Try to notice how other people deal with problems, too and note whether or not you feel that they use any of the mental mechanisms described above. They are often easier to spot in other people!

KNOW YOURSELF   Questions about this section

1	I do not think that I use mental mechanism at all	SA	A	U	D	SD
2	Its not particularly healthy to look at yourself so closely	SA	A	U	D	SD
3	I think that I am fairly honest with myself and others	SA	A	U	D	SD

■ APPROACHES TO SELF-AWARENESS

In the last section of this chapter, we consider two other approaches to developing self-awareness: through using the Johari Window and through an approach developed out of Transactional Analysis. It is worth experimenting with a wide range of self-awareness methods. It is important to find one that suits you and not all methods suit everyone. Try the exercises in this section and compare these approaches with ones discussed so far.

The Johari Window

The Johari Window was devised by Jo Luft and Harry Inghams: the name of the window is taken from their first names [21]. The window offers a fairly straightforward means of exploring aspects of the self and is illustrated in Fig. 2.2

The model is made up of four sectors:

- The Open Area
- The Blind Area
- The Hidden Area
- The Unknown Area

	Known to self	Not known to self
Known to others	Open Area	Blind Area
Not known to others	Hidden Area	Unknown Area

Figure 2.2. The Johari Window.

The open area is easily described. It is that part of us that *we* know about ourselves and that *others* know about us. Thus both I and my family know that I am fairly tall, reasonably hard working and rather moody. No particular secrets here!

The blind area is that part of us that *others* know about us but of which we are unaware. Thus, my colleagues at work presumably have some opinions of me that I do not know and can therefore neither agree nor disagree with. I can only become aware of these 'blind' aspects as others disclose their view of me, to me.

The hidden area contains all of those things that I do not tell others about. Thus part of me remains hidden to others. It is notable that I am not hidden equally to all other persons. There are people, such as my family, who know 'more' about me and people who are acquaintances that know very little.

The unknown area is that hypothesised area that is both unknown to me and unknown to others. It remains uncharted territory. Luft's argument is simply this: that we can come to know more about our hidden selves as we either (a) disclose more of ourselves to others (Fig. 2.3) or receive feedback about ourselves from others (Fig. 2.4). Under the conditions of both self-disclosure and feedback from others, we can 'grow' considerably in the unknown area (Fig. 2.5). Luft argues that we can all enhance our sense of self and get to know our selves and others better if we take the risk in disclosing ourselves and if we are prepared to hear other people's assessment of us.

Whilst the Johari Window is particularly useful in group settings, the following exercise offers you some ways of exploring your concept of self, using the Johari model.

	Known to self	Not known to self
Known **to** **o**thers	Open Area	Blind Area
Not **k**nown **to** **o**thers	Hidden Area	Unknown Area

Figure 2.3. The Johari Window following self-disclosure.

	Known to self	Not known to self
Known **to** **o**thers	Open Area	Blind Area
Not **k**nown **to** **o**thers	Hidden Area	Unknown Area

Figure 2.4. The Johari Window following feedback from others.

	Known to self	Not known to self
Known t**o** **oth**ers	Open Area	Blind Area
Not k**no**wn **t**o **oth**ers	Hidden Area	Unknown Area

Figure 2.5. The Johari Window following both self-disclosure and feedback from others.

EXERCISE	**Number 18**
Aim of exercise:	To explore the self using the Johari Window
Activity:	Rule up a large sheet of paper into four quadrants. Number them as follows:

1 The Open Area
2 The Blind Area
3 The Hidden Area
4 The Unknown Area

Take your time over this exercise and jot notes in each of the four sections as follows:

1 The Open Area. Write notes in the following order:
(a) Things about myself that I have no difficulty in telling others
(b) Things about myself that I have some difficulty in telling others

2   The Blind Area. Write notes, here about how you imagine the following people see you:
(a) Your best friend
(b) One of your patents
(c) Someone (named) who doesn't like you very much
(d) A colleague at work
(e) Someone you have nursed recently

3   The Hidden Area. Write notes, here, about things that you *would not* disclose to others.

4   The Unknown Area. Switch off the logical, 'thinking' part of you and write notes, here, about what you are really like underneath the layers of self that you present to both yourself and others. What could surprise you about yourself? What would surprise others about you?. This is obviously the most difficult area to write about but have a go.

When you have made notes in the four sections, reflect on what you have written and consider the following issues:

● What would happen if you allowed more people to know you?
● How could you find out more what others think about you?
● What surprises were there when you did this exercise?
● To what degree are you self-disclosing by nature?

Variations: The Johari Window is obviously well suited to exercises that take place between pairs of people or in groups. Consider undertaking a variation of the above activity with a trusted friend.

First, rule up two sheets of paper in four quadrants, as described above. Then, you and your friend both fill in the section headed 'Open Area'. In this section, write notes about what you have little difficulty in disclosing to others.

Then exchange sheets and fill in the section marked 'Blind Area'. In this section, each of you tries to honestly describe the others.

Third, and this is the most difficult part, take back each of the sheets and try to write a couple of items under the 'Hidden Area', heading. In other words, try to write down some things about yourself that your friend is unlikely to know about you. Then exchange sheets and reflect on each others partially completed windows. Discuss your findings and notice the degree to which you learned more about yourself in the process. What you learn will enable you to move into the 'Unknown Area'. Notice, particularly, what it *feels* like to do this activity. Consider whether or not you could do the same exercise with a larger group of people.

I'm OK – You're OK

Transactional Analysis is a reasonably straightforward development of Freudian psychodynamic theory. It was thought out by Eric Berne [22]. One part of that theory suggests that we can adopt at least four orientations towards other people and the world at large. Whichever orientation we adopt will colour the ways we see ourselves, the way we see others and the way we treat and react to others. The four orientations are as follows:

- I'm OK – You're OK
- I'm OK – You're not OK
- You're OK – I'm not OK
- You're not OK – I'm not OK

I'm OK – You're OK. This is the orientation of the person who is fairly much at home with herself and therefore accepting of other people. She tends to find that she is positive both about herself and about the people she meets.

I'm OK – You're not OK. This is the orientation of the person who is not comfortable with herself but disowns the uncomfortable feelings and 'sees' them, instead, in other people. This is the person who is highly critical of others whilst remaining silent about her own shortcomings.

You're OK – I'm not OK. This is the groucher. This is the person who feels sorry for herself and notices that most other people manage quite well whilst she has to struggle.

You're not OK – I'm not OK. This is the unhappiest position of all. This person finds little acceptable in herself and in turn finds other people fairly disagreeable. This person has a negative view on life in general.

EXERCISE	**Number 19**
Aim of exercise:	To explore aspects of self from the point of view of an aspect of Transactional Analysis
Activity:	On a sheet of paper, jot down the names of people who fit the following descriptions:

- A close friend
- A person you do not like
- A teacher in your College of Nursing
- A patient that you have nursed recently
- A senior colleague at work
- One of your parents

Next to each of these names, write down the orientation that seems to fit them best.

Then read through the list and the orientations and decide which orientation fits *you* best. Which of the following positions best describes *you*?

- I'm OK – You're OK
- I'm OK – You're not OK
- You're OK – I'm not OK
- You're not OK – I'm not OK

Now consider the degree to which you are happy with this position, what caused you to adopt it and whether or not you want to change it. If you do want to change, plan out a strategy for that change. What will you have to do to review your outlook on life and other people? Can you do it alone or will you need help from other people?

KNOW YOURSELF **Questions about this section**

1	Generally, I have a fairly positive outlook on life	SA	A	U	D	SD
2	I am usually positive at work but less so at home	SA	A	U	D	SD
3	People can change fairly easily if they really want to	SA	A	U	D	SD

■ **OTHER METHODS OF DEVELOPING SELF-AWARENESS**

So far, we have considered a variety of approaches to self-awareness. There are many other ways of finding out more about yourself. Here is a list of some other methods of developing self-awareness. Read through it and note the methods that *you* tend to use and the ones that you rarely, if ever use. Notice, too, any methods that you would not normally associate with self-awareness and consider how *you* could learn from them. The list is drawn from other things that other nurses have said have increased their self-awareness.

Talking to other people
Listening to others
Meditating
Listening to music
Writing poetry
Keeping a diary
Counselling
Psychotherapy
Group activities

Drama
Psychodrama
Chanting
Singing
Educational activities
Moving home
Tai Chi
Martial arts
Hobbies

Sporting activities
Looking at art
Travelling
Reading
Relaxing
Changing job
Listening to other people's evaluation of you
Psychoanalysis
Dream analysis
Prayer
Yoga
Playing music
Painting
Writing stories
The Alexander Technique
Sexual activities

Spending time by the sea or in the country
Evening classes
Learning a language
Aromatherapy
Massage
Cathartic work
Assertiveness training
Doing something different
Transactional analysis
Gestalt therapy
Co-counselling
Encounter group work
Body work
Problem solving
Running

■ PROBLEMS IN SELF-AWARENESS DEVELOPMENT

Finally, a note of caution: self-awareness development is fraught with problems. Some of the main ones are identified here.

The Guru Problem

First, people who run self-awareness groups are sometimes charismatic people who inspire those who attend their groups. This may be true of weekend workshop facilitators and of some nurse educators. This can have both good and bad effects. The positive side is that such people can enthuse and inspire people to develop themselves and get to know themselves better. The less positive side is that such people can create dependence in others. If self-awareness means getting to know yourself better as a unique individual, it is important that you do not get too dependent on other people – particularly on charismatic leaders. Dependence, after all, can never be compatible with autonomous thinking and acting.

The Problem of Smugness

Some people who develop self-awareness become big-headed. They feel that being self-aware is about being slightly superior to the other mere mortals that inhabit the planet. It is arguable that such people are not all that aware at all. Self-awareness tends to bring humility and an understanding of human frailty both in self and in others.

The Painful Aspect

Finding out about yourself often involves some pain. If we explore the darker side of ourselves, as outlined above, the process is *definitely* painful. One of the problems is that we often want to explore ourselves without anything changing. But to develop self-awareness is *necessarily* to change: you cannot know yourself more without being different as a result. The secret, here, is two-fold. First, proceed slowly and at your own rate. Second, keep a sense of humour. You do not have to be earnest and meaningful all of the time. If you maintain a sense of fun you will not only find out quite a lot about yourself but you will also enjoy doing it.

A New Language

As with all groups, the human potential or personal growth movement (which accent the need for self-awareness) has tended to choose to use a certain type of jargon. Thus, you may come across people concerned with self-awareness who use expressions such as these:

- 'May I share something with you . . . ?'
- 'Can I check something out with you . . . ?'
- 'May I invade your space . . . ?'

I feel that it is not necessary to learn a new language in order to become self-aware. There is a curious paradox about people who talk in this way. They are advocating getting to know themselves as individuals and yet they all tend to talk in the same sort of way!

The Overwhelming Nature of the Task

The real question is this: is it *possible* to get to know yourself? This may sound like a thorny philosophical question and it is. If it is the self that is under scrutiny, then it is also the self that is doing the scrutinising. Can a 'thing' observe *itself* in this way? In the strict sense, probably not. On a lighter note, though, it seems reasonable to suppose that in getting to notice our thoughts, feelings and behaviours we are going some way to understanding ourselves a little more.

These are a few of the problems associated with the issue of self-awareness. Whilst none of them are incapacitating, all should be borne in mind in order to keep things in perspective. Probably the most important thing to keep in mind is the issue of a sense of humour. If *that* goes, you might as well give up the whole project. No one who is very self-aware but devoid of a sense of humour is likely to be of great help to others.

■ SUMMARY OF THIS CHAPTER

This chapter has discussed various aspects of self-awareness. It has considered:

- An integrated model of self-awareness
- Self-awareness and nursing
- How we fool ourselves
- The Johari Window and its use as a self-awareness tool
- Eric Berne's description of four orientations towards the world
- Other methods of developing self-awareness
- Some problems in self-awareness development

3 | The Thinking Approach

I still live, I still think; I must still live, for I must still think. I wish to be at all times hereafter only a Yea-sayer.

F. NEITZSCHE

All that we are is the result of what we have thought.

BUDDHA

Keywords	• Thinking
	• Note-taking
	• References
	• Databases
	• Writing
	• Critical thinking

Aims of this chapter	• To explore the concept of thinking
	• To explore ways of examining your thinking
	• To help you structure your thinking in practical situations

In the previous chapter we explored an integrated model of self-awareness. It was noted that part of the inner aspect of self could be divided up into four: the thinking aspect, the feeling aspect, the sensing aspect and the intuiting aspect, after Jung's typology of the mind. In this chapter, the thinking aspect is explored in some detail. Also, your *use* of thinking is explored. It is one thing to think: it is another to make good use of that thinking.

▮ THINKING

Your Thinking Style

What is thinking? In a sense, the question is redundant for we all know what it is. Just to reflect for a moment on what goes on inside you head is to know about thinking. What is noticeable, when you do just that, is that thinking is not necessarily a *linear* process: we do not always think in a logical, ordered fashion. Instead, our thinking often darts from one thing to another. Some writers have attempted to capture this 'flow of consciousness' in their novels. See, for examples of this, James Joyce's *Ulysses* and

Virginia Woolf's *To the Lighthouse*. Note the degree to which you feel these writers *have* managed to capture the flavour of how we think. Probably it is impossible to capture exactly the fluctuations, cul de sacs and switches involved in thinking. John Chilton Pearce [23] has referred to this as 'roof brain chatter'. Just stop reading for a moment and notice how you are not just concentrating on this chapter but also simultaneously thinking of many other things at the same time.

EXERCISE	**Number 20**
Aim of exercise:	To explore aspects of your thinking
Activity:	On a sheet of paper try to jot down all the things that go through your mind. Try to leave nothing out and do not try to 'order' the material in any way. Notice if you have a tendency to go blank after a short while and notice what it was you were thinking about when this happened.
Variations:	Once you have jotted down thoughts in this way for a period of about 4 minutes, you may like to try to reorganise them. Do they seem to fall into a particular pattern or are they fairly random? Do certain themes predominate? Notice, too, the degree to which you *like* to order your thoughts. Some people tend to be *serial* thinkers and like to take a logical and tidy approach to thinking things through. Other people tend to be more *holistic* in their thinking and pay less attention to detail and logic and more to a whole cluster of various thoughts. How would you describe your thinking?

Confusion in Thinking and Arguing

One of the ways we demonstrate how we think is how we *argue*. Daniels and Horowitz [24] identify five typical problems that people run into when they argue:

- Begging the question
- Loaded labelling
- Questionable assumption
- Straw person
- Suppressed information

Begging the question means endorsing without proof the actual question that is at stake: 'We have to go to the party because that's what we are doing this evening'. With loaded labelling, facts and value judgements become mixed. With this ploy, it is difficult to know whether the speaker is offering fact or his own opinion. When we make questionable assumptions, we go beyond the facts or mix one fact with another to produce a curious hybrid: 'She doesn't get on with patients because she doesn't like surgical nursing'. Using a straw person argument means distorting someone's views and then attacking the person on the basis of that misrepresentation. 'Orem's model of nursing is faulty because of it's psychodynamic orientation and psychodynamic approaches can never be proved conclusively'. When we suppress information, we only offer the information that is available to use if it suits us.

If we can learn to be more clear in the way we argue and when we debate, we are well on the way to clarifying our thinking. Faulty argument will only ever lead to more of the same.

	KNOW YOURSELF! **Questions about this section**					
1	I often notice flaws in other people's arguments	SA	A	U	D	SD
2	I only argue if I am sure I am right	SA	A	U	D	SD
3	It is important for me to be right in an argument	SA	A	U	D	SD

Remembering and forgetting

In order to continue thinking we need to be able to remember! There are three well-recognised effects that hinder remembering [25]:

- The 'Von Restorff' Effect
- The Primacy Effect
- The Recency Effect

The Von Restorff effect describes how we remember unusual events. For instance, you may have forgotten a lot of what one of your lecturers has said in her lectures but you will remember what she was talking about when she dropped all her notes on the floor. Another example is when we remember what we are doing when something catastrophic happens. For example, we often remember what we were doing when we heard a TV report that someone famous had died. You can sometimes aid your own remembering by linking what you have to learn with something odd. Thus if you have to remember a book title, try to associate the title with something related but slightly bizarre. I often remember them by conjuring up a picture of their cover and remember the *colour* of the cover, before I remember the title.

With the primacy effect, we tend to remember the first two of three things that we are told during a learning session or at a conference, then we progressively 'turn off'.

This is why all learning is more effective if it is broken into small chunks. Then more and more items are the 'first' ones!

The recency effect is almost the polar opposite of the primacy effect. Here, we tend to remember the *last* few things that we are told and tend to forget the items that went before. Sometimes, too, the last things that you learn *replace* previous pieces of learning.

It becomes clear that for effective remembering we need to keep learning sessions short so that there are lots more beginnings and ends. We also need to try to link what we learn the odd images, thoughts or visualisations.

■ HOW DO YOU USE YOUR THINKING?

Now we turn to ways of organising thoughts. It is one thing to have great thoughts: it is another to structure them so that they can be used:

One of the problems, for many people, is developing a way of routinely and clearly structuring what they think about. There are three elements that are regularly needed by all students:

- A structure for keeping references
- A structure for taking notes
- A structure for writing essays and reports

EXERCISE	Number 21
Aim of exercise:	To explore the ways that you organise your thoughts

Activity:	Find two pieces of your written work: one piece that has been written fairly recently and one that was written some time ago. If possible, find two pieces that have been marked by a teacher or lecturer.

Read through these two pieces and note to what degree the following are true:

- The writing is clear and easy to read
- The paper is divided up by headings
- There are at least two paragraphs on each page
- Your style of quoting references is consistent
- Your work begins with a description of what is to come and ends with a summary of what has gone before

When you have read through your work in this way, reflect on what changes you could bring to bear on what you have written and how you might improve your written work.

Variations:	If you have the opportunity, try to read a colleague's work, using the above criteria. If you can, compare your work and try to discuss some of the things that could improve the clarity of presentation.

Note Taking

Most people have to take notes occasionally. Occasionally is the word, though. You may notice how frequently people sit through lectures or conferences trying to jot down every word that has been spoken. This is usually a recipe for disaster. No one can listen, write and understand at the same time. Wherever possible, try to find out whether or not the information being given at a lecture of conference is available in the form of handouts. If not, take notes judiciously and develop a *system* of note taking. Two examples are offered here.

The first is the well known spider's web approach devised by Tony Buzan [26]. With this approach, you do not attempt to write everything down. Instead, you note the various themes to the lecture and develop an increasingly elaborate 'spider's web' that allows you to relate various points. Figure 3.1 illustrates one example of such a web. The topic of the lecture, here, was 'counselling in nursing'. It is suggested that this approach more nearly approximates the way we think. As was noted above, we do not think in a linear fashion: thinking tends to far less organised than that. The spider's web approach to note taking allows you to see a whole range of thoughts at once – on one page. The disadvantage of this approach is that you end up with a fairly untidy set of notes.

An alternative and much more orderly approach is the one offered in Fig. 3.2. Here, each separate issue addressed in a lecture is dealt with as a separate 'block', either side of the page. In this way, it is easy to glance down the page and quickly get the gist of what a lecture was about. Also, the 'white space' that is created between paragraphs allows you to go back and edit your notes with additions and references.

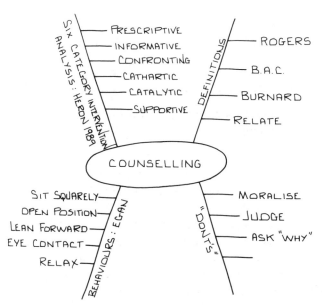

Figure 3.1. An example of the Spider's Web approach to note taking.

```
┌─────────────────────────────────────────────┐
│                 Counselling                  │
│                                              │
│  Definition                                  │
│  Counselling is a process through            │
│  which one person helps another to           │
│  explore and solve their own life            │
│  problems.                                   │
│                                              │
│                    Counselling Skills        │
│                    Counselling skills may be │
│                    separated into two:       │
│                    (1) Attending and listening│
│                    and                       │
│                    (2) Counselling interventions.│
│                                              │
│  Attending                                   │
│  Attending refers to the                     │
│  process of focusing                         │
│  away from your own concerns                 │
│  and directing your attention                │
│  onto the other person.                      │
│                                              │
│                    Listening Skills          │
│                    First, the behavioural    │
│                    skills of listening:      │
│                    Egan (1986) S.O.L.E.R.     │
│                    S = sit squarely          │
│                    O = open position         │
│                    L = lean forward          │
│                    E = maintain eye contact  │
│                    R = relax                 │
└─────────────────────────────────────────────┘
```

Figure 3.2. Example of a systematic approach to note taking.

Which style you adopt is your own decision. What is more important is that your style remains *consistent*. Most people are familiar with the process of collecting reams of notes which are then either unreadable afterwards or are never referred to again! Keeping clear notes is one way of organising your thinking and will allow you a much more systematic approach to writing essays and papers.

Whether or not you rewrite your notes is a matter of personal preference. Some suggest that it is a bit of a waste of time. If you write clearly enough in the first place, there should not be any need to rewrite. Another point of view, though, is that the process of rewriting serves to reinforce learning.

If you use a computer and a wordprocessor, you may want to use the function known as 'outlining' both to organise your notes and to prepare essays and papers. An outliner in its most simple form is a means of generating headings. You then go back an add sub headings and sub-sub headings. In this way, you gradually build up a more and more detailed plan or set of notes. For example, you may start a set of notes on groups as follows:

Groups
1 Types of groups
2 Group life
3 Group dynamics
4 Facilitating groups.

You then go back to those headings and add another 'layer':

1 Types of groups
   (a) primary
   (b) secondary
   (c) therapy
   (d) work
   (e) open
   (f) closed.

2 Group life
   (a) forming
   (b) storming
   (c) norming
   (d) performing

3 Group dynamics

And so on. Obviously, you can also do this with a pad and pencil. Computerised outlining, though, allows you to quickly change the order of your headings and sub headings. It also allows you to go back and fill in the details under each heading. This way, you produce a neat and orderly set of notes or a very detailed plan for an essay. Various outlining packages are available for most sorts of computers [27].

Another way of organising your thoughts without the use of a computer is by using cards. If you are trying to organise material for an essay or project, jot down each idea as it comes to you onto a separate index card. The handiest size for this purpose is 5" × 3". Make out a separate card for each idea. When you have jotted down all the ideas that come to you, organise the pile of cards into an appropriate order. One way to do this is to sort them into a series of piles according to topic. Then the various piles will give you the structure of your paper or project. Alternatively, lay the cards out on a table and move them into vertical rows. With this method, you can freely move topics from one row to another and you can see how all your ideas link up.

Storing References

Another way of organising your thoughts is by linking them to the thoughts of other writers. Most nursing and other courses require that you reference your work when you write essays, project work and research reports. It is important to become systematic in your keeping of references. As you read, you need to have some way of keeping track of the details of the book or journal article, for future reference.

One way of doing this is through the keeping of a card system. Many people use plain index cards of the 8″ × 3″ variety. These can then be laid out in a standard format as shown in Fig. 3.3. The example shows the layout for a book. The order of the layout for a journal article is shown in Fig. 3.4. As each card is filled in it can be filled away, alphabetically by author in a plastic index box.

Increasingly, people are using computers to prepare essays and projects. In this case, it is useful to keep your references on computer. Various database programs are available and can be used in a similar way to the card index described above [28]. The added advantage is that, given the right program, all of the references appropriate to a particular project can be pulled out and printed at the end of your work, without the need for your writing them out again. The keyword, here, is simplicity. Aim for a database that is simple to operate and to develop. I use one that is part of a hard-disk organiser. It is very simple but so far I have collected more than 700 references in it and can call up the appropriate articles and books in 1–2 seconds. Initially, I used a well known and expensive program that could do far more but which nearly drove me mad whilst trying to work out how to use it! The same format and layout as shown in Figs 3.3 and 3.4 can be used with a computerised database system.

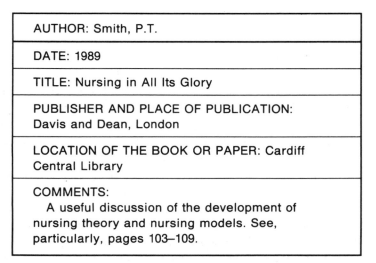

Figure 3.3. Example layout of a reference card for a book.

```
┌─────────────────────────────────────────────────┐
│ AUTHOR: Jones, R.A. and Black, M.N.             │
├─────────────────────────────────────────────────┤
│ DATE: 1989                                      │
├─────────────────────────────────────────────────┤
│ TITLE: Nursing Past and Present: A Review of the│
│ Literature                                      │
├─────────────────────────────────────────────────┤
│ PUBLISHER AND PLACE OF PUBLICATION:             │
│ Nursing Standard, Vol 3, No. 4. Pages 24–26.    │
├─────────────────────────────────────────────────┤
│ LOCATION OF THE BOOK OR PAPER: College of       │
│ Nursing Library                                 │
├─────────────────────────────────────────────────┤
│ COMMENTS:                                       │
│   A literature review that will be useful for the│
│ final year project.                             │
└─────────────────────────────────────────────────┘
```

Figure 3.4. Example layout of a reference card for a journal article.

EXERCISE	**Number 22**
Aim of exercise:	To examine your own referencing system
Activity:	Review the way that you collect and store references. Could you be more methodical? Or do 'overcollect' and write cards for every article or book that you ever see? Do you have a system for quickly locating references when you need them and do you regularly 'prune' your reference system?
Variations:	If you have not yet started a referencing system, buy some cards and a box today!

Layout of Essays and Papers

Next, the issue of how you organise your thoughts on paper. A full discussion of how to write essays and papers is beyond the scope of this book (and other books are available which do this well [29]). Here, we are concerned with two things:

● How your paper should be laid out
● How you should use references

Figure 3.5 offers an example of the layout of one page of an essay. Note the following aspects of it:

● The use of clear headings and sub headings
● The use of paragraphs

Counselling and Nursing

Jane Smith

Nurses have increasingly recognised the need for counselling skills in their nursing care. This essay explores some of the skills required. It then discusses the role of counselling in nursing and closes with a brief examination of how nurses might be training in counselling.

Counselling Defined

Not all writers define counselling in the same way. Black (1) in his discussion of counselling in the social services suggests that it is :

> '...helping people to identify and explore their problems with a view to changing their behaviour..'

In a nursing context, White (2) has defined counselling in terms of a range of skills and interventions. She writes that counselling involves listening to people and not intruding with your own thoughts, beliefs and values.

In summary, counselling can either be thought of as a process or as a set of skilled that can be used to offer the patient help with his or her problems of living. In the next section, some of the skills involved in counselling are explored.

Counselling Skills

Two sorts of counselling skills are identified in the literature (3,4) : listening skills and counselling interventions. Listening skills are those that involve our giving our complete attention to the other person. They also involve taking note of both what the other person is saying and how they are saying it.

Figure 3.5. An example of the layout of an essay.

- The use of indenting for all paragraphs after the first one in each section
- The use of double spacing
- The use of short sentences
- The use of references (The Vancouver system is used here)

You can ignore the *content* of the example: the important thing is the *layout!* This form of layout can be used for both handwritten and wordprocessed essays and papers. If you use a wordprocessor, remember, again, to keep it simple. Whilst double spacing is important for ease of reading and marking, there is no need to use fancy typefaces, fonts or graphics. Such things often get in the way of the content. The use of wordprocessors is, on the one hand, an advantage in that you never have to totally rewrite anything again. On the other hand, they have such a wealth of features that it is always tempting to overdo the use of devices simply because they are there. Also, because wordprocessing is simple, you can be tempted to generate an awful lot of words. The secret is to go back and edit fairly frequently rather than be seduced by the ease of producing text.

When it *does* come to the content, bear in mind what the sociologist C. Wright Mills wrote many years ago:

> To overcome the academic *prose* you have *first* to overcome the academic *pose*. [30]

The best writing is clear and simple. The writer does not try to be clever for the sake of it. Simplicity, as someone once said, is genius.

EXERCISE	Number 23
Aim of exercise:	To review the layout of your own writing
Activity:	Find an essay or project that you have written. Ignore the *content* of the paper. Instead, study it from the point of view of its *layout*. Note whether or not you use any of the following:

- Clear headings and sub headings
- Short paragraphs
- Indenting for all paragraphs after the first one in each section
- Double spacing
- Short sentences
- Correct referencing (check with your department or College, here; different institutions and publishing houses have different preferences about which style or referencing you should use)

Then find an published article from a referred journal (the *Journal of Advanced Nursing* or *Nurse Education Today*, for example) and note how those papers are laid out. Compare *your* style with the style of the published paper and reflect on whether or not you could modify your layout to make it clearer.

Variations: You may want to do this as a group activity. If you can bear it, allow other people to look at your work and review the work of others. Again, note only the layout and not the content.

Referencing

Two styles of referencing are popular: the Harvard System (Fig. 3.6) and the Vancouver system (Fig. 3.7). Your college may prefer to use one or the other. The important thing is to be consistent and to use only one of them. Mixing of the two styles does not help in making your work readable.

The point of referencing your work is to show that you have a clear grasp of the literature related to the field about which you are writing. References also allow the

The Harvard System of Referencing
In the Text:
Brown (1987) suggested that all of the nurses in her study were uncertain about their level of assertiveness. This was in keeping with the findings of White (1985), Green and Davis (1978) and Matthews (1986).
At the end of the paper:
Brown, P. 1987 Assertiveness and nurses: a comparative study: *Journal of American Nursing*: 3: 4: 234–237.
Green, D. and Davis, T. 1978 Nurses in conflict. *Nursing Weekly*: 4: 6: 134–146.
Matthews, S. 1986 Are nurses assertive? *Journal of Registered Nurses*: 3: 1: 45–52.
White, F. 1985 Nursing and change. *Journal of Clinical Nursing*: 2: 3: 56–58.

Figure 3.6. Elements of the Harvard system of referencing.

The Vancouver System of Referencing
In the Text: Brown (1) suggested that all of the nurses in her study were uncertain about their level of assertiveness. This was in keeping with the findings of other researchers (2,3,4,5,).
At the end of the paper: 1. Brown, P. 1987 Assertiveness and nurses: a comparative study. *Journal of American Nursing*: 3: 4: 234–237. 2. White, F. 1985 Nursing and change. *Journal of Clinical Nursing*: 2: 3: 56–58. 3. Green, D. and Davis, T. 1978 Nurses in conflict. *Nursing Weekly*: 4: 6: 134–146. 4. Matthews, S. 1986 Are nurses assertive? *Journal of Registered Nurses*: 3: 1: 45–52.

Figure 3.7. Elements of the Vancouver system of referencing.

EXERCISE	**Number 24**
Aim of exercise:	To explore the use of styles of referencing
Activity:	Find four nursing journals: two of the 'referred' variety and two of the weekly 'magazine' type. Look through them and note the style of referencing that those journals use. You will usually find that each journal is consistent in its use of references. What advantages and disadvantages in the use of the Harvard and Vancouver systems? Which would you use by choice?
Variations:	Explore a variety of textbooks and note the styles of referencing used in them.

Counselling and Nursing

Jane Smith

Nurses have increasingly recognised the need for counselling skills in their nursing care. This essay explores some of the skills required. It then discusses the role of counselling in nursing and closes with a brief examination of how nurses might be training in counselling.

Counselling Defined

Not all writers define counselling in the same way. Black (1) in his discussion of counselling in the social services ('Counselling in the Social Services', Thompson and Andrews, London, 1986) suggests that it is :

> *'...helping people to identify and explore their problems with a view to changing their behaviour..'*
> *(BLACK 1986)*

In a nursing context, White (1989) has defined counselling in terms of a range of skills and interventions. She writes that counselling involves listening to people and not intruding with your own thoughts, beliefs and values.

In summary, counselling can either be thought of as a process or as a set of skilled that can be used to offer the patient help with his or her problems of living. In the next section, some of the skills involved in counselling are explored.

Counselling Skills

Two sorts of counselling skills are identified in the literature (Green, P. The Art of Counselling) : listening skills and counselling interventions. Listening skills are those that involve our giving our complete attention to the other person. They also involve taking note of both what the other person is saying and how they are saying it.

Figure 3.8. How not to use references.

reader to follow up some of the points that you have made in your work. If you are clear and consistent in your use of references, that process of finding the works that you have referred to is that much easier. Figure 3.7 demonstrates the main differences between the two systems. Both have their advantages and disadvantages. As a general rule, the Harvard system is the one preferred by referred journals and by lecturers in colleges. On the other hand, the Vancouver system allows for a 'cleaner' essay, with fewer interruptions for the reader. It is not uncommon to find people mixing styles when they are unsure of how to use references. Figure 3.8 offers an example of such mixing. The overall impression is one of lack of clarity.

KNOW YOURSELF! **Questions about this section**

1	There are important differences between published papers and the sort of papers I am asked to write	SA	A	U	D	SD
2	I need to be more careful about my use of references	SA	A	U	D	SD
3	Presentation does not matter: its the content that counts	SA	A	U	D	SD

Becoming a Critical Thinker

It is not sufficient that we believe all we hear or read. More important is the ability to discriminate between what is rational, research based, logical and well argued, on the one hand, and that which is only opinion or not well argued, on the other. This is not to dismiss other people's views altogether but to acknowledge, with Carl Rogers [31] that 'I can trust my experience' and 'evaluation by others is not a guide for me'. Here, the accent is on finding out for one's self: of testing out established theory through one's own experience.

Earnest Hemingway suggested that all students should develop what he called 'shock-proof crap-detectors'. He felt that it was all too easy for other people to be taken in by what was written in books or by what was being declaimed by teachers. Hemingway suggested that from an early age, students should be encouraged to challenge what they heard or read. In a more academic fashion, Stephen Brookfield [32] has proposed the following list of characteristics of the critical thinker:

- Identifying the challenging assumptions is central to critical thinking
- People who think critically try to imagine and explore alternatives
- Imagining and exploring alternatives leads to 'reflective scepticism'

	KNOW YOURSELF! Questions about this section					
1	I'm critical enough already	SA	A	U	D	SD
2	I do not like to be critical of people who I think know more than me.	SA	A	U	D	SD
3	I do not mind being critical of anything or anyone	SA	A	U	D	SD

■ SUMMARY OF THIS CHAPTER

This chapter has explored various aspects of thinking. Specifically, it has considered the following issues:

- Thinking style
- Confusion in thinking and arguing
- How you use your thinking
- Note taking
- Storing references
- Using references
- Improving the layout of your writing
- Becoming a critical thinker

4 | The Feeling Approach

Poetry is the spontaneous overflow of powerful feelings: it takes its origin from emotion recollected in tranquillity.

W. WORDSWORTH

Keywords	<ul><li>Feelings</li><li>Bottled-up feelings</li><li>Expressing feelings</li></ul>
Aims of this chapter	<ul><li>To explore feelings</li><li>To examine feelings and nursing</li><li>To help you identify how you deal with your own feelings</li></ul>

■ WHAT ARE FEELINGS?

We are all aware of having feelings when something extreme happens. If we are very upset or very happy, then we can usually acknowledge our feelings fairly readily. Sometimes, though, we suddenly realise that all sorts of feelings are going on just beneath the surface. Someone says something to us and we suddenly get angry. We hear a piece of music and find ourselves near to tears. In this chapter we explore a whole range of facets of feelings. The two main hypotheses here are that (a) we all have hidden feelings and (b) we are usually better off identifying and releasing our feelings.

EXERCISE	**Number 25**
Aim of exercise:	To identify the feelings that you associate with *you*
Activity:	Read through the following list of words that describe feelings. Identify the ones that you *do* associate with yourself and those that you do not. Notice, too, the feelings that you would *like* to experience and those that you would rather not.

accepting	extrovert	relaxed
adventurous	fit	resentful
aggressive	friendly	responsible
ambitious	frightened	sad
angry	guilty	secure
anxious	happy	settled
apathetic	humiliated	shy
appreciative	hurt	stressed
appreciated	hurtful	strong
assertive	indecisive	superior
attractive	independent	supporting
bashful	inferior	supported
bold	insecure	suspicious
bored	interested	tense
burnt-out	introvert	trusting
bright	involved	unambitious
cautious	irresponsible	unappreciated
cheerful	jealous	unassertive
competitive	joyful	unattractive
confident	lonely	uneasy
confused	loved	unfriendly
cooperative	loving	unloved
cynical	optimistic	unlovable
daring	outgoing	unwanted
decisive	pessimistic	vulnerable
dependent	powerful	wanted
depressive	powerless	weak
discontent	rejected	worried
embarrassed	rejecting	worthless
energetic		

Variations:

Notice the degree to which you identify *positive* and *negative* feelings. As a general rule, do you tend to see yourself in a positive or a negative light? How do you think others see you? Do they concur with your image of yourself or do you think they view you in quite a different light? If so, who is right. Notice the mental gymnastics that can occur here. It is quite possible for a person to publicly acknowledge that she is fairly hopeless, only to have this view argued with by a friend or colleague. Secretly, she is both pleased to hear the affirmation and also, secretly, prepared to believe that the other person is right!

THE NATURE OF FEELINGS

Heron [33] distinguishes between at least four types of emotion, that are commonly suppressed or bottled up: anger, fear, grief and embarrassment. He notes a relationship between these feelings and certain overt expressions of them. Thus, in counselling, anger may be expressed as loud sound, fear as trembling, grief through tears and embarrassment by laughter. He notes, also, a relationship between those feelings and certain basic human needs. Heron argues that we all have the need to understand and know what is happening to us. If that knowledge is not forthcoming, we may experience fear. We need, also, to make choices in our lives and if that choice is restricted in certain ways, we may feel anger. Thirdly, we need to experience the expression of love and of being loved. If that love is denied us or taken away from us, we may experience grief. To Heron's basic human needs may be added the need for self respect and dignity. If such dignity is denied us, we may feel self-conscious and embarrassed.

THE EFFECTS OF BOTTLING UP FEELINGS

Physical Discomfort and Muscular Pain

Wilhelm Reich, a psychoanalyst with a particular interest in the relationship between emotions and the musculature noted that blocked emotions could become trapped in the body's muscle clusters [34]. He noted that anger was frequently 'trapped' in the muscles of the shoulders, grief in muscles surrounding the stomach and fear in the leg muscles. Often, these trapped emotions lead to chronic postural problems. Sometimes, the thorough release of the blocked emotion can lead to a freeing up of the muscles and an improved physical appearance. Reich believed in working directly on the muscle clusters in order to bring about emotional release and subsequent freedom from suppression and out of his work was developed a particular type of mind/body therapy, known as 'bioenergetics' [35].

Trapped emotion is sometimes 'visible' in the way that a person holds himself and the skilled nurse can learn to notice tension in the musculature and changes in breathing patterns that may suggest muscular tension. We have noted throughout this book how difficult it is to interpret another person's behaviour. What is important here is that such bodily manifestations be used only as a clue to what may be happening in the person. We cannot assume that a person who looks tense, is tense, until he has said that he is.

You will be very familiar with the link between body posture, the musculature and the emotional state of the person. Frequently, if patients and clients can be helped to relax, then their medical and psychological condition may improve more quickly. Those health professionals who deal most directly with the muscle clusters (remedial gymnasts and physiotherapists, for example) will tend to notice physical tension more readily but all carers can train themselves to observe these important indicators of the emotional status of the person in their care. Consider, for a moment your own muscular status? Do you feel tense? What does that tension tell you? Keleman [36] posed these questions:

> What attitude are you meeting the world with right now? . . . Cautious and distancing? Depressed and withdrawn? Bombastic and outgoing? Identify the attitude with which you greet the world, and locate it somewhere in your body. Is it in the back of your neck? Is it in your eyes? Is it in your stomach or in your shoulders or in your knees? Wherever you locate it . . . notice how it shapes your thoughts and actions, your self and your responses.

EXERCISE	**Number 26**
Aim of exercise:	To explore tensions in your body
Activity:	Lay down on the floor and take a few deep breaths. Now systematically work through your sets of muscles from your head and face, down through your shoulders and arms, your trunk and abdomen and finally your hips and legs. Notice which parts of you are relaxed and which parts are tense. Now pick a tense area and explore it a little. If, for instance, the tension is in your shoulders, try massaging your shoulders a little. Notice any emotion that you feel as you do this. Then, do something different: try to *exaggerate* the tension that you feel. Notice the emotion that you feel as you do this. Then, pose yourself the leading question: what is this tension about? . . .

Difficulty in Decision Making

This is a frequent side effect of bottled up emotion. It is as though the emotion makes us uneasy and that uneasiness leads to lack of confidence. As a result, we find it difficult to rely on our own resources and find decision making difficult. When we are under stress of any sort it is often the case that we feel the need to check decisions with other people. Once some of this stress is removed by talking through problems or by releasing pent up emotions, the decision making process often becomes easier.

EXERCISE	**Number 27**
Aim of exercise:	To explore your own decision making
Activity:	This one is easier. Just reflect for a few minutes on your own decision making processes. Do you make decisions easily? *All* decisions? Do you tend to ask lots of people what *they* think before you make decisions? Are decisions sometimes easier to make at certain times than at others?

Faulty Self-Image

When we bottle up feelings, those feelings often have an unpleasant habit of turning against us. Thus, instead of expressing anger towards others, we turn it against ourselves and feel depressed as a result. Or, if we have hung on to unexpressed grief, we turn that grief in on ourselves and experience ourselves as less than we are. Often, as old resentments or dissatisfactions are expressed, so the person begins to feel better about himself. Notice how easy it is to bottle up feelings that lead to our convincing ourselves that we are not very good/intelligent/lovable.

EXERCISE	**Number 28**
Aim of exercise:	To explore your relationships with yourself and with others
Activity:	Read through, and silently complete, the following sentences:

- The person I resent most is . . .
- The person I respect most is . . .
- The person I would like to be like is . . .
- I think that I am . . .
- Other people think that I am . . .
- I would like to be more . . .
- I wish I was not so . . .
- I would be a better person if . . .
- The thing I would most like to change about myself is . . .

Setting Unrealistic Goals

Tension can lead to further tension. This tension can lead us to set ourselves unreachable targets. It is almost as though we set ourselves up to fail! Sometimes, too, failing is a way of punishing ourselves or it is 'safer' than achieving. Release of tension, through the expression of emotion can sometimes help in a person taking a more realistic view of himself and his goal setting.

The Development of Long Term Faulty Beliefs

Sometimes, emotion that has been bottled up for a long time can lead to a person's view of the world being coloured in a particular way. He learns that 'people can't be trusted' or 'people always let you down in the end'. It is as though old, painful feelings lead to distortions that become part of that person's world-view. Such long term distorted beliefs about the world do not change easily but may be modified as the person comes to release feelings and learns to handle his emotions more effectively.

The 'Last Straw' Syndrome

Sometimes, if emotion is bottled up for a considerable amount of time, a valve blows and the person hits out – either literally or verbally. We have all experienced the problem of storing up anger and taking it out on someone else: a process that is sometimes called 'displacement'. The original object of our anger is now replaced by something or someone else. Again, the talking through of difficulties or the release of pent-up emotion can often help to ensure that the person does not feel the need to explode in this way.

Summary

Clearly, no two people react to the bottling up of emotion in the same way. Some people, too, choose not to deal with life events emotionally. It would be curious to argue that there is a 'norm' where emotions are concerned. On the other hand, many people complain of being unable to cope with emotions and you perceive there to be a problem in the emotional domain, then that perception may illustrate a need to explore your emotional status. A variety of methods is available to help in the exploration of the domain of feelings and those methods will be described. Sometimes, these methods produce catharsis: the expression of strong emotion: tears, anger, fear, laughter. Drawing on the literature on the subject, the following statements may be made about such emotional release:

- Emotional release is usually self-limiting. If a person is allowed to cry or get angry, that emotion will be expressed and then gradually subside. Nothing awful will happen.

- Once a person has released emotion they will need time to piece together the insights that they gain from such release. Often all that is needed is that a friend sits quietly with you while you verbalise what you are thinking.

- There seems to be a link between the amount we can 'allow' another person to express emotion and the degree to which we can handle our own emotion. This is another reason why nurses need self-awareness. To help others explore their feelings we need, first, to explore our own. Many colleges and university departments offer workshops on cathartic work and self-

awareness development that can help in both training the
counsellor to help others and in gaining self-insight.

EXERCISE	**Number 29**
Aim of exercise:	To explore situations in which you express or hide your feelings
Activity:	Read through the following situations and note in which of them you allow yourself to express feelings or you hang on to them.

- During a concert
- At a wedding
- When someone else is upset
- When you are at the cinema
- When someone in your family gets angry
- When a patient cries
- Never!

	KNOW YOURSELF Questions about this section					
1	I am not really a very emotional person	SA	A	U	D	SD
2	People should keep their emotions under control	SA	A	U	D	SD
3	I would like to be able to express my emotions more easily	SA	A	U	D	SD

■ TO CONTROL OR RELEASE FEELINGS?

Should you release or control your feelings? There is no easy answer to this. Probably,
the answer goes something like this. It is unlikely to do you a lot of good to bottle
up emotions all the time. As we noted above, bottling up of emotions leads to all sorts
of emotional and physical problems. On the other hand, it is usually inappropriate to
express emotions every time we feel them. The point is probably to develop the skill
of *noticing* what is happening to our emotions. If we can notice when we are upset and
agree to explore that upset with a friend later on, we are more likely to benefit than
if we merely move on and forget all about the upset.

Later in this chapter, we explore some ways of helping to release bottled up emotion. If the premise is accepted that we all have bottled up feelings, then it will be clear that at some time we will all need to express feelings. Some people have no problems in this department – they can express feelings easily and appropriately. Others, though, find considerable difficulty in expressing how they feel. The ways identified below can help.

KNOW YOURSELF   Questions about this section

1	Crying about something rarely helps	SA	A	U	D	SD
2	In our society, we tend to block off a lot of our feelings	SA	A	U	D	SD
3	I can handle my own feelings fairly well	SA	A	U	D	SD

■ FEELINGS AND NURSING

For a long time, the prevailing norm in nursing was that nurses should control their feelings. If patients or their relatives became upset it was the nurse's duty to remain calm, placid and unemotional. Meg Bond has described this situation well in her book *Stress and Self Awareness*, as has Jane Salvage, in a different way in her *Politics in Nursing*. The problem with this calm and placid approach was that nobody seemed to take into account what nurses did *after* they had appeared calm and placid. It was assumed, I suppose, that nurses remained untouched by the emotional situations they found themselves in.

The climate is slowly changing. It is being recognised that nurses have feelings and that they need to express them. The following exercise invites you to explore your perceptions of the emotional domain in nursing.

EXERCISE	**Number 30**
Aim of exercise:	To explore how you cope with your feelings in nursing
Activity:	Read through the following situations and identify how you normally react to them:
1	A child on a paediatric ward begins to cry. Do you: (a) feel upset yourself? (b) rush to comfort her?

(c) wonder what to do?

(d) handle the situation calmly?

2 A relative has been told of the death of one of your patients and that relative gets upset. Do you:

(a) put your arm round her?

(b) cry with her?

(c) find yourself reminded of your own partings?

(d) handle the situation easily?

(e) try to find someone else to help the relative?

3 A colleague gets very upset because she has failed her examinations. Do you:

(a) tell her that everything will work out in the end?

(b) suggest that she should have studied harder?

(c) allow her to cry?

(d) find yourself wondering what to say?

All of these situations call for certain skills in coping with the person who is upset. They also tend to generate feelings in *us*. The important things are (a) letting other people express what they feel and (b) being able to recognise our *own* feelings as they arise. We may not be able to express our feelings there and then, but, as we noted above, we can always work through them later with a friend or in a support group.

KNOW YOURSELF   Questions about this section

1	Nurses are still not encouraged to express their feelings	SA	A	U	D	SD
2	The best nurses are those that can hide their feelings	SA	A	U	D	SD
3	Some nurses are very good at helping patients to express their feelings	SA	A	U	D	SD

■ METHODS OF EXPLORING FEELINGS

These are practical methods that can be used to identify, examine and, if required, release emotion. They can be used simply by reading through the description of them and then trying them out, in one's mind. Alternatively, they can be tried out with a colleague or friend. Another way of exploring their effectiveness is to use them in a peer support group. If you can find a group of supportive colleagues and perhaps a nurse or teacher who has had experience of running groups, it may be possible to set such a group up in your area. All of the following activities should be used gently and thoughtfully and timed to fit in with your current needs. There should never be any sense of pushing yourself to explore feelings because of a misplaced belief that 'a good cry will do me good!'

Giving Permission

Sometimes we try desperately to hang on to strong feelings and not to express them. This may be due to the cultural norm which suggests that holding on is often better than letting go. Thus a primary method for exploring your emotions is for you to give yourself permission for the expression of feeling. This can be done simply through acknowledging that 'It's alright you feel you are going to cry . . .'.

Literal Description

This is one to use with a friend or colleague. When you are feeling emotional but unable to express the emotion, notice what or who you are talking about. Then describe that place or person in detail as if it, or the person, were in front of you. This often has the effect of making the emotions surface.

Locating and Developing a Feeling in Terms of the Body

Start to notice where, in terms of your body, you experience emotion. Do you, for example find that your throat gets tight when you are close to tears? Do you feel tension in your stomach when you are anxious? One way of exploring emotion is to notice these physical sensations and then try to *exaggerate* them. This, again, often has the effect of bringing the emotion to the surface. Sometimes, though, it does just the opposite – the emotion goes away completely! This can also be used to your advantage. If you find that this happens, next time you feel stressed, allow yourself to become *more* stressed. Then notice how you seem to calm down almost at once. It seems as though, if we give ourselves permission to feel things, unpleasant feelings turn out to be not so bad after all. It is often when we try to *fight* emotions that we find them difficult to deal with.

Contradiction

This is related to the previous idea. Here, instead of allowing a feeling, you try to contradict it. This is particularly useful when you 'know' that you are denying feelings. For example, if you are prone to say to yourself 'I feel fine, everything is OK' and you are fairly sure that they are not, try making a contradictory statement. Sometimes, such a statement will allow the 'real' feelings to emerge.

Mobilisation of Body Energy

If you are feeling emotionally 'stuck', try taking vigorous exercise – running or swimming, perhaps. Then notice the emotion emerge as you undertake this exercise and try to identify what it is about. You can use the rest of the run or the swim to work the emotion out of your system.

Exploring Fantasy

We often set, fairly arbitrary, limits on what we think we can and cannot do. When you seem to be doing this, it is sometimes helpful to explore what may happen if this limit was broken. What would happen if you *allowed* yourself to do something or feel something? As you reflect on this, you will often find that this 'allowing' process takes the sting out of the way that you are feeling.

Rehearsal

Sometimes the anticipation of a coming event or situation is anxiety provoking. It is helpful to try to role play or rehearse a situation that you know is likely to cause you upset. You can do this in one of two ways. First, you can play through the scene in your mind and try out different sorts of approaches. Even better, you can role play the anticipated event with a friend or colleague, where that person plays the 'antagonist'. This works even better if you encourage the person to play 'devil's advocate' and give you as bad a time as possible! All this rehearsal allows you both to air your feelings and to practice the reponses that you can use in the real situation.

Summary

These are just some of the ways that you can explore your own feelings. Others are described in the literature on counselling and psychotherapy – particularly Gestalt therapy and you may want to read more about these [37].

As we have noted, it is often better to explore your feelings in the company of someone you like and trust. One format for doing this is the co-counselling approach. In co-counselling, you set aside a set amount of time each week (say 2 hours). Then, for the first hour, *you* talk through your thoughts, feelings and anything that has been worrying you during the week. During this hour, your friend merely listens to you and tries neither to interrupt nor offer advice. After this first hour, roles are reversed and you listen while your friend works through her own thoughts, feelings and problems. Once again, there are various books on the topic of co-counselling which you may want to read [38]. Courses in co-counselling methods are also held in various extra-mural departments of colleges and universities. One such department is the Human Potential Resource Project at the University of Surrey, Guildford.

■ SUMMARY OF THIS CHAPTER

This chapter has been about feelings and how you cope with them. It has considered the following:

- What feelings are
- How you cope with feelings
- What happens when you bottle them up
- Feelings and nursing
- How to explore your feelings

5 | The Sensing Approach

Everything has its beauty but not everyone sees it.

CONFUCIUS

If facts are the seeds that later produce knowledge and wisdom, then the emotions and the impressions of the senses are the fertile soil in which the seeds must grow.

RACHAEL CARSON

Keywords	● Senses
	● Noticing
	● Seeing
	● Hearing
	● Touch
	● Taste
	● Smell

Aims of this chapter	● To examine the five senses
	● To identify ways that your senses can help you in nursing

■ THE FIVE SENSES

The five senses are obvious to all of us: seeing, hearing, touching, tasting, smelling. Not all of us have equally developed senses, though all are important both personally and in our work as nurses. The more that we can notice the world outside of ourselves the more we also become aware of our inner world: the two complement each other. If we spend too long looking inwards, we get a confused picture of who we are. We need to develop a sense of balance between the outer and inner experience.

The other point about the senses is this: that arguably everything that is inside our heads came to us through the senses. We experience the world and what we know about it through reference to the senses. Everything we know, we heard, saw, tasted, touched or smelled. Unless, that is, we accept the notion of intuition . . . and that is the focus of the next chapter. At the moment, the focus is on the five senses.

This chapter offers a series of activities through which you can explore the senses.

■ ATTENDING AND NOTICING

These are two important skills that can be developed consciously and used in all branches of nursing. Attending refers to the notion of closely listening to other people and hearing what it is that they say and noticing what it is they do. All that you are required to do is attend. What we often do instead is one of two things: either we do not attend very well at all and only half listen to others. Or we hear and notice but draw all sorts of *conclusions* about what the other person *means*. The point, here, is to suspend all judgment and merely listen. This is not nearly as easy as it seems. It is second nature to most of us to filter, judge, agree or disagree with what other people say to us. To learn to listen without these sorts of mental processes taking place can not only help us to *really* listen. It can also help us to be more therapeutic in our relationships. Often what other people need is not judgment or agreement but simply someone to hear them.

Noticing refers to the notion of simply paying attention to what is going on around you. You are not asked to form judgments about what you see or hear but merely to *notice*. Again, this is not particularly easy. We tend to 'tag' what we see with labels such as 'attractive', 'ugly', 'pleasant' and so on. When we do this, what we are *not* doing is noticing things just as they are. Again, the skill of attending in this way is one means of really paying attention to what is happening around you. This can mean that we become better at observation in general and possibly less judgmental of both our surroundings and of other people. This is not to suggest that we should lose all of our critical faculties but merely to suggest that the starting point for understanding ourselves and the world is to *notice what is there*.

The ability to notice and to not rush to name what we see or to judge it is an important one in all aspects of nursing. Usually, we seem to have an inbuilt censor inside our heads which labels things as 'right', 'wrong', 'good' or 'bad'. As we listen to other people, the censor continues to make its judgment. If we are not careful, the censor begins to make *overall* judgments about people. Thus we find ourselves labelling *people* as good or bad, right or wrong. These labels are often developed out of the flimsiest of evidence and they are labels that, once given, tend to stick. We are likely to be more open minded and more balanced in our perceptions if we resist the censor — at least until more of the evidence has emerged. This process is a *vital* one in the fields of counselling and psychotherapy and in most aspects of mental health nursing.

EXERCISE	**Number 31**
Aim of exercise:	Exploring all of your senses
Activity:	Sit quietly, on your own and take a couple of deep breaths. Then allow your attention to focus on your senses. Take note of what you can taste, touch, smell, hear and see. Notice how, normally, you filter out a lot of what is going on around

---

you and how you are often unaware of sounds and sights that are very close to you. Allow you attention to focus on each of the senses in turn and notice the degree to which it is easy or difficult to focus on more than one of the senses at a time. As you do this exercise, notice how your attention moves *away* from what is going on inside your head (your thoughts and feelings) and how your breathing tends to slow down. This activity can also be used as a form of stress relief and as a way of 'winding down' at the end of a difficult day.

KNOW YOURSELF   Questions about this section

1	Certain of my senses are better developed than others	SA	A	U	D	SD
2	I often find that I am so caught up with my thoughts and feelings that I do not notice what is going on around me	SA	A	U	D	SD
3	I feel that I am generally fairly observant	SA	A	U	D	SD

▮ SEEING

EXERCISE	**Number 32**
Aim of exercise:	To explore aspects of the visual sense
Activity:	Stop what you are doing and look around you. Just sit and allow yourself to notice everything that enters your visual field. Do not attempt to evaluate what you see nor even attempt to 'name' what you see. Just allow yourself to notice everything that your eye wanders over. Notice how, normally, your attention is so caught up with other things that you do NOT notice things around you. Continue to do this for about 5 minutes. After about 5 minutes, stop and consider what you have been doing. What was it like to just sit and notice? How did it *feel* to carry out this activity? What, if anything, did you *think* about as you did it? How much visual input do you normally miss because your mind is so preoccupied with other things? How could increasing your visual awareness

help in your nursing practice? Could you learn to become more attentive to your surroundings? Could you improve your observational skills by practising this activity?

| Variations: | 1 | Allow your attention to focus on just one object and study it in considerable detail for about 5 minutes. |
| | 2 | Notice the limits of your visual field. Look straight ahead for a few moments and notice *how much* you can see. Notice, particularly, your *peripheral* field of vision. Notice how much you can see without moving your head. Consider this in relation to talking to a patient. As you are looking at his face you are also taking in a whole range of other data about him: his non-verbal behaviour, his colour, his expression, his clothes and so on. |

EXERCISE	**Number 33**
Aim of exercise:	To explore the visual sense through meditation (1)
Activity:	Sit quietly in a place where you are not likely to be disturbed. Have in front of you an object that you can look at. You may choose a painting, a statuette, a piece of rock or a flower. Simply sit in front of it and concentrate your full attention on it. Examine it, visually, in detail. Then allow your attention to take in the whole of it. If you become distracted, simply return to the object of contemplation. As you contemplate, allow your breathing to slow down a little and also feel yourself relax. Continue contemplating the object for at least 10 minutes.
Variations:	On the second or third attempt at this meditational activity, you may want to ask yourself as many questions as you can about the object of contemplation . . . where did it come from? . . . who made it? . . . what is its history? . . . how have similar objects been used in history? . . . what are its links with literature or poetry? . . . and so on.

EXERCISE	**Number 34**
Aim of exercise:	To explore the visual sense through meditation (2)
Activity:	This is similar but different to the previous activity. For this meditation you will need a lighted candle. Again, find yourself a quiet place where you are not likely to be disturbed.

Place the lighted candle in front of you and concentrate your attention on the flame. Concentrate on nothing else and if your attention wanders, gently bring it back to the object of contemplation. Continue the activity for at least 10 minutes. This activity not only develops the visual sense but is also a powerful way of helping to combat stress. As a meditation, it has been used in Yoga and by Hindus and Buddhists [39].

EXERCISE	**Number 35**
Aim of exercise:	To explore 'seeing in a different way'
Activity:	We tend to get used to things that we see around us. So much so, that we often fail to notice them at all. This is a simple, if at first odd, exercise.
	Sit quietly on your own and look around you. Then look closely at things upon which your gaze falls. Try to see them *without naming them*. In other words, you may be looking closely at a tree. Instead of just noticing that it is a tree, look closely at it and describe it in detail without naming it and the parts of it in the usual way. If you can do this, you can get to see very familiar things in a new light and notice details that you never saw before.
Variations:	Try this with people! Observe people that you know *as if you did not know them*. Look closely at them and describe their features to yourself but imagine that this is a first meeting. Again, notice what you take for granted and what this 'new way of seeing' reveals.

EXERCISE	**Number 36**
Aim of exercise:	To explore seeing in a different way with another person
Activity:	This is a variant of the exercise above. To do this one you will need to work with another person. Sit in a room together and study objects that you see around you. Then, have one of you describe in some detail, an object in the room, without referring to its usual name or function. In other words, you may be looking at a picture on the wall and your description may sound a little like this:

'. . . It is a large square object. The edge is surrounded by a thin gold strip. In the centre is a rough surface covered in various colours. All of the colours seem to form a pattern . . .' and so on.

After one of you has described some objects in this way, in some detail, have the other do the same.

Here is the self-awareness twist to this exercise! After you have got the hang of this exercise, begin to describe the object from the point of view of the 'first person'. In other words, start to describe objects using the word 'I'. If you were describing the picture, for example, you would start:

'I am a large square object . . .'

Notice what those descriptions *mean* to you or what they *say about you*. An odd side effect of this exercise is that when we describe things in this way, we often notice qualities in the things around us that are also aspects of ourselves. This may sound odd to read about. Try it out! See what happens! To give you some clue as to what can happen, this is one person's description of a living room chair:

'I am large and fairly comfortable. A lot of people sit on me. Sometimes I get out of shape and then people push me around until I get sorted out . . .'

Perhaps our perceptions of the world at large are more coloured by our feelings and thoughts about ourselves than we first imagine. If you can, carry out this activity in pairs, but within a group context. Have the group reform and discuss what you discovered when you described things from the point of view of 'I'.

This is an exercise adapted from those developed in Gestalt Therapy. Many other similar but different exercises of this sort can be found in the literature on Gestalt therapy [40] and you may want to explore some of them.

▮ HEARING

Often, in everyday life, we filter out many of the sounds that are around us. This is often necessary. If no filtering took place it would be difficult to concentrate on what we are doing. Stop reading for a moment and concentrate on your sense of hearing. Try to notice all the sounds that you can. Then notice how much you were unaware of prior to doing this exercise. What happens to what you are thinking and feeling when you concentrate hard on listening?

How good a listener are you with other people? Listening is an essential aspect of nursing care. To listen to another person is to begin to develop empathy with them, to enter their frame of reference. Often, if we are preoccupied with our own thoughts and feelings we find ourselves unable to truly listen to others. Yet listening is a skill that you can learn. You can simply make a contract with yourself to give time to others. During that time, you undertake to listen to them carefully and allow them to talk. Notice as you do this any tendency you may have to be a 'sentence finisher' for others – a sure sign that you are either not listening very well or that you are growing impatient. Try to slow down a little, relax and give yourself more fully to the other person.

EXERCISE	**Number 37**
Aim of exercise:	To explore the aural sense
Activity:	Find yourself a room in which you can be alone to listen to music. Find a cassette or a record of a piece of music that you like. Try to choose a longish piece that takes at least 10 minutes to be played.
	Then play the piece through twice and listen to it in two different ways. First, listen to it from the point of view of the *emotional* effect that it has on you. Notice the parts that you particularly like and those that pass you by fairly easily. Notice, too, any emotions that the piece invokes.
	Then play the piece through a second time but listen to it in a very different way. Listen to the *structure* of the piece. Notice, for example, how it is orchestrated and how instruments are used in it. Notice the main themes and how these are dealt with by the person who wrote it. As you listen to it in this analytical way, notice how your response to the piece differs from when you listened to it from the point of view of its emotional effect.
	Whilst you are doing this exercise, notice the degree to which you can or cannot fully concentrate on the music. Are you, for instance, distracted by other sounds or sights? Are you drawn away from the music by what you are thinking or feeling. Notice all of these things and then return to the task in hand.
Variations:	Try this double sided approach to listening to music that you hear on the television and radio. Sometimes listen from the point of view of the music's emotional effect and sometimes listen to the structure. Then begin to notice *how* the structure of a piece of music affects the emotional content. In the end, the two aspects are not so separate after all but inextricably linked.

EXERCISE	**Number 38**
Aim of exercise:	To explore the aural sense through meditation
Activity:	Find a quiet place where you are unlikely to be disturbed. Sit quietly and let your focus of attention settle on any pleasant or neutral sound that you can hear. Concentrate only on this one sound. If the sound changes, allow your attention to move with the sound. Adopt a relaxed and passive attitude to distractions. If you find your attention wanders, gently bring it back to the sound that you are concentrating on. Try to just listen and try not to 'judge' the sound in terms of whether or not it is loud or soft, harsh or gentle, good or bad. Just listen.
Variations:	A difficult variation on this activity is to sit in a quiet place and listen to the sounds that occur *inside your head*. To do this, take a few deep breaths, close your eyes and allow your concentration to focus internally. For most people, this exercise is initially very difficult and it is easy to become distracted by thoughts and feelings that emerge. If this happens, try to return gently to the process of listening to 'internal' sounds.

EXERCISE	**Number 39**
Aim of exercise:	To explore listening to another person
Activity:	This activity requires that you have a friend or colleague with you. The exercise is in two parts. Try to do both.

First, decide who is going to talk first and who is going to listen. Then, the talker talks for about five minutes whilst the 'listener' does not listen at all! The talker can talk about any topic that she chooses. After 5 minutes, switch roles and have the listener do the talking and the talker take the role of the 'non-listener'. Notice (a) what it is like to talk to someone and to have them ignore you, and (b) notice what it is like to sit and ignore someone.

Second, repeat the exercise, with each person taking 5 minutes to talk. This time, though, the listener listens! Note that this is not a conversation. Only one person talks at a time and the listener does just that. After 5 minutes, notice what it was like to have someone's full attention and what it was like to be allowed to talk for a full 5 minutes. |

Compare the quality of your listening in this exercise with the quality of your listening in other aspects of your life and work.

EXERCISE	**Number 40**
Aim of exercise:	To explore your effectiveness as a listener
Activity:	Read through the following items and rate yourself according to what you do when you listen to other people. Use the following scale:

    0 Never
    1 Very rarely
    3 Sometimes
    4 Very often

What you do when you listen	Score
Pretend to listen whilst actually thinking of other things	
Finish other people's sentences for them	
Moralise and tell people what they *should* do	
Find yourself getting angry with other people	
Wish that people would listen to *you* more	
Interpret what people say and tell them what they *really* mean	
Label or diagnose other people	
Blame others for what happens to them	
Advise other people	
Be surprised at what other people say	
Refuse to accept other people's feelings	

Variations:	You may want to do this exercise in a small group and discuss the outcomes. Try to identify what you *could* do in place of the items listed above. What would be more therapeutic and helpful?

■ TOUCH

Touch is an important aspect of nursing work. Whilst we are often touching patients in our work it is interesting to ponder on the degree to which we do or do not like to be touched ourselves. The world can probably be divided into 'high touchers' and 'low touchers'. Some people confuse touching that is nurturing and friendly with touching that is sexual in nature. When they do this, they often tend to avoid touching others altogether in any sense other than the sexual, in case the meaning of the touch is mistaken. In this way, they lose out on a lot of affection.

Obviously, touching others and being touched is only one aspect of the sense of touch. It is, however, a vital one. Much of our communication with others is through the sense of touch. Indeed, much of our interaction with the world is via this sense. When we eat food, wash, change, sit down and so on, we are experiencing the world through touch.

EXERCISE	**Number 41**
Aim of exercise:	To explore the degree to which you allow others to touch you
Activity:	Write a short list, in the following order:

1	People whom I have no hesitation in letting touch me
2	People whom I am wary of letting touch me
3	People whom I would never let touch me
4	People I would like to touch me more

Are you a high or low toucher? How did you get to be this way? If you are a low toucher, would you like to touch and be touched more? What would happen if people touched you more?

Variations:	In some educational and therapy groups, it is quite common for people to hug each other, either as a sign of welcoming or saying goodbye, or when a member of the group is distressed in some way. Sometimes people just hug in groups because they like to! You may or may not want to experiment with touch in this way. Notice whether or not the idea appeals to you or repels you.

■ TASTE AND SMELL

Of all the senses, those of taste and smell are often the most undeveloped. Yet they are the senses that we rely on considerably at an almost unconscious level. Obviously we use them when we eat but we also use them when we relate to others: we often *smell* people! This is not to suggest that most people have unpleasant body odour but that often (particularly when sexual chemistry is involved) we become aware of how another person smells. Now to the more personal issue: how do *you* smell? Can you be sure that when you are working with patients that you always smell clean? If you are a smoker, are you careful to brush your teeth before returning to work with clients?

EXERCISE	**Number 42**
Aim of exercise:	To explore the senses of taste and smell
Activity:	Take an orange or another sort of fruit that you particularly like. Simply take your time chewing and eating it. Notice the degree to which smell and taste are linked. Notice, too, how tastes change as you continue to chew.
Variations:	Try to turn off your other senses and note what you can taste or smell in your immediate environment.

■ THE SENSES AND NURSING

As we have already noted, the senses play an important role in all aspects of nursing. We need to be observant in order to help identify patient needs and wants. We also need to remember that the patient *also* experiences the world through his or her senses. One of the people that he or she sees is you. What do you look like to him or her? Are you aware of how you appear to others? Do you consciously develop an awareness of your expression, the way you hold yourself, the way you dress? This is all part of the conscious use of self discussed in the first chapter. In order to be able to help people optimally, we need to consider how we *appear* to them.

There is something very difficult about all this. On the one hand, we are often being urged to 'be natural'. On the other, we are being asked to notice ourselves and pay attention to what we do. The net result, initially, is often embarrassment and self-consciousness. Perhaps we *have* to go through such a stage if we are to become really aware of ourselves. Fortunately, the stage does not usually last very long. If we can begin to notice how we present ourselves to others and experiment with making slight changes, after a while, the 'new presentation of self' becomes 'natural' again and we no longer feel awkward and self-conscious.

This process of becoming more aware in this way seems to go through three stages. In stage one, we do not think at all about noticing what we do — we simply do it. In the second stage, we begin to become aware of what we are doing and become self-conscious as a result. The greatest temptation, at this stage, is to give up the activity altogether. If we can stick it out to the third stage, however, the process of noticing ourselves in this way becomes 'second nature' and part of the natural repertoire of what we do. When we reach this stage, we have successfully incorporated the skill of self-noticing into our behaviour. It has become part of who we are.

1	I do not think *how I look* matters very much. It is what I am *like* that counts	SA	A	U	D	SD
2	I do not expect that people like looking at me very much	SA	A	U	D	SD
3	People who are aware of how they look tend to get self-centred and conceited	SA	A	U	D	SD

■ SUMMARY OF THIS CHAPTER

This chapter has considered the domain of *sensing*. It has explored aspects of the senses and how we might use our senses more effectively in the delivery of nursing care. Specifically, it has explored:

- Attending and noticing
- Seeing
- Hearing
- Touch
- Taste and smell
- The senses and nursing

6 | The Intuitive Approach

I cannot say it,
I cannot know it,
I cannot be it,
Because I am it,
And all it is I am.

WEI WU WEI

Heard melodies are sweet, but those unheard are sweeter . . .

KEATS

Keywords	● Intuition
	● Synchronicity
	● Meditation
	● Focusing
	● Journals
	● Dreams
Aims of this chapter	● To explore intuition
	● To examine ways of becoming more intuitive

■ WHAT IS INTUITION?

Intuition is a difficult thing to define but we probably all acknowledge that we have it. In one way, it is 'knowledge beyond the senses'. Sometimes, it seems we just 'know' things, without first having heard or seen them. Think for example of the following situations:

● You are thinking of a friend and she rings you
● You are about to say something, in a conversation, quite unrelated to what has been talked about before, and the person you are with goes to say the same thing
● You ask just the right sort of question of someone at just the right time
● You anticipate, correctly, something that is about to happen

Arguably, in each of these cases, a degree of intuition is occurring: we are going beyond the already known. There may not be anything particularly mysterious about intuition. Some people feel that when we demonstrate intuition we go through the normal thinking processes but at an accelerated rate: we miss out some of the stages in thinking. Because of this, the thoughts that occur to us seem to come to us out of the blue. On the other hand, some people feel that intuition *does* have a mysterious element to it: what do *you* think?

However it is explained, intuition is an important part of most of our lives. We depend, for example, on being able to anticipate what the people we live with are going to do or say, in a general sort of way. If we did not, every day would come as something of a shock to us! In nursing, the intuitive domain is one that we can use to enable us to be more sensitive to the needs of our patients. When we are intuitive, we move beyond the exercising of professional, well rehearsed skills towards acting in a natural and compassionate way, based on what we 'sense' is required at the time. The American psychotherapist Carl Rogers said that he functioned at his best as a counsellor when he forgot his skills and allowed intuition to guide him [41]. Benner [42] in her description of the 'expert practitioner' in nursing seems to be suggesting something similar when she argues that the skilled nurse acts 'by the seat of her pants'. She no longer has to consciously think about what to do as a nurse: she just does it.

The psychologist, Carl Jung [43] used the term *synchronicity* to describe a certain sort of intuitive experience. Synchronicity is 'meaningful coincidence'. Not everything that happens coincidentally is meaningful. For example, as I am writing this, coincidentally, the washing machine in the kitchen has just started a new cycle: hardly 'meaningful'! On the other hand, events do seem to occur that suggest that some coincidences are more than just 'chance' occurrences. Consider, for example, the following scenarios. Have they ever happened to you?

- You are puzzling over a particular problem and you browse, by chance, through a book and come across the solution
- You become interested in a new topic and suddenly you meet another person who has the same interest
- You are thinking of a piece of music and suddenly you hear it played on the radio or TV

Pure chance, you may say. On the other hand, it is worth noting how frequently such 'chance' happenings occur. Just becoming aware of synchronous events can help in the process of developing intuition. There are many links to be made between what happens in our minds and what happens in the 'outside' world. The knack is noticing that they happen at all. The mystic, George Gurdjieff, argued that we spend most of our lives 'asleep' [44]. He suggested that we fail to *remember ourselves*. Remember, for example, occasions on which you have walked or driven some distance and then have no recollection of how you got from A to B. Gurdjieff would suggest that this is an example of forgetting ourselves or failing to 'stay awake'. The more we can notice, perhaps, the more we will see [45].

EXERCISE	**Number 43**
Aim of exercise:	To explore your reaction to the notion of intuition
Activity:	All you are required to do here is to think about intuition and the degree to which you 'believe' in it. Do you feel that you often exercise intuition? Are there certain situations in which you are more intuitive than others? Are you more intuitive with certain people?
	Alternatively, do you dismiss the notion of intuition altogether, maintaining that it is just another form of thinking? Jung [3] argued that the person who was basically a 'thinking/sensing' type, tended to be dismissive of intuition, preferring the world of logic and 'hard facts'.

Given that we have noted how difficult it is to define intuition, it is going to be relatively hard to find ways of developing it! However, we can put ourselves into the right psychological state to encourage the likelihood of our being able to exercise intuition. If, for example, we are constantly tense and preoccupied, we are unlikely to be at our most intuitive. In the exercises that follow, we explore four approaches to developing intuition: meditation, focusing, the keeping of a journal and dream analysis. If you have not come across any of these methods before, try to suspend judgment on them until you have read the following sections and try the exercises that are offered. All of the exercises will increase the likelihood of your getting to know yourself a bit better and thus increase self-awareness. The meditation exercises take a little time to get used to and require practice. It is helpful if you can try to spend 10–15 minutes of each day practising meditation and to continue this practice for at least three weeks before you make your mind up about whether or not meditation helps you.

KNOW YOURSELF   Questions about this section

1	Intuition is something that either happens or it does not; you cannot encourage it	SA	A	U	D	SD
2	I think that I am fairly intuitive	SA	A	U	D	SD
3	Intuition is a mystery and as such should be left alone	SA	A	U	D	SD

■ MEDITATION

One approach to developing intuition is through contemplation and thoughtfulness, via meditation. In the normal flow of life we are constantly being caught up in the processes of thinking about our work, our families, our commitments and so on. Meditation has been used for centuries for mystical, religious and secular purposes. There are many excellent accounts of the history and theory behind various meditational practices [46]. The following activities are simple and effective. They can be used to explore self-awareness or they can be used simply as a means of inducing relaxation. They can be used by the individual or by a small group. They are described as though they relate to the individual meditating on her own. If they are used in a small group setting, it is advisable to find a room where people can be undisturbed and quiet. It is also probably better if the facilitator does not try too hard at invoking a 'mysterious' atmosphere. As we noted above, meditation takes a little working at and some practice.

EXERCISE	Number 44
Aim of exercise:	To practice a simple calming technique
Activity:	Close your eyes and concentrate on holding your mind quite steady but do not feel any urgency or tension about doing this. At first, you may only achieve this holding for a few moments. As you practice, however, it is possible to begin to calm the mind and to 'hold' it for longer periods. Initially, the 'roof brain chatter' that Pearce [47] describes will tend to crowd in and distract you. Roof brain chatter is the whole stream of thoughts and ideas that tends to rush through our mind as soon as we start to reflect on that mind.
Variations:	A second method involves the holding of a simple object that you can cup in your hand. Hold the object and attempt to confine your attention to it. If your thoughts start to wander, slowly bring them back to the object. Again, allow yourself to acknowledge and be distracted by the roof brain chatter, at first. As you become more used to the activity you will find it possible to concentrate on the object for longer periods.

EXERCISE	Number 45	
Aim of exercise:	To attempt the activity known as 'noticing the breaths'	
Activity:	1	Sit motionless, comfortably and with the eyes closed.
	2	Breath quietly and gently. Breath in through the nostrils and out through the mouth.

3 Let your attention focus on your breathing.
4 Begin to count your breaths, from 1 to 10. One is the whole cycle of an inhalation and an exhalation. Two is the next complete cycle.
5 When the breaths have been counted from 1 to 10, begin to count the next set from 1 to 10 and so on.
6 If you are distracted or lose count, simply go back to the beginning and start again.

EXERCISE	**Number 46**
Aim of exercise:	To explore a 'guided fantasy' meditation
Activity:	Lie on your back with your hands by your sides . . . stretch your legs out and have your feet about a foot apart . . . pay attention to your breathing . . . now let your breathing become gentle and relaxed . . . now I want you to experience your body growing in size . . . your head, your arms, your legs, your trunk . . . are all growing in size . . . experience that sense of growing and allow yourself to grow more . . . experience your growing until your head reaches the top of the ceiling . . . feel your vastness . . . and experience a feeling of calmness and equanimity . . . now continue to grow . . . your head goes up into the sky . . . until all the surrounding town and countryside is contained within you . . . you are continuing to grow . . . you grow larger still . . . feel your vastness . . . until your head is amongst the planets and you are sitting in the middle of the galaxy . . . the earth is lying deep inside you . . . feel all this and experience the feeling of vastness . . . of awe . . . of calmness . . . sit in this universe . . . silent, huge, peaceful . . . continue to grow . . . until you contain all galaxies . . . you are at one with everything . . . experience the vastness . . . let everything be as it is . . . the silence . . . . Now, very slowly, allow yourself to return . . . come down in size slowly . . . past the galaxy . . . down, slowly to the size of the earth . . . now slowly to the surrounding countryside and towns and notice all that is around you . . . now continue to come down in size until you fill the room, slowly, gently . . . now return to your normal size . . . and just lie for a while and experience the sense of peace and relaxation . . . think of your experience . . . remain quiet and relaxed . . . take a couple of deep breaths . . . in your own time . . . slowly stretch . . . sit up gently . . . and open your eyes.

■ FOCUSING

Related to meditation, but also different to it, is the process known as focusing. This is a simple process of allowing the body and mind to relax and thus enabling a 'felt sense' of one's problems to emerge. The process can also encourage the development of the intuitive side to our personalities. The focusing approach outlined here is based on that described by Eugene Gendlin [48].

EXERCISE		**Number 47**
Aim of exercise:		To explore 'focusing'
Activity:	1	Sit quietly and breath deeply for a while. Allow yourself to relax completely. Notice the thoughts and feelings that flood into your mind. Slowly, but without worrying too much, identify each one.
	2	Having identified each thought or feeling that comes drifting into your mind, find some way of 'packaging up' each of those thoughts and feelings. Some people find it easiest to imagine actually wrapping each issue up into a parcel. Others imagine putting each item into a box and sealing it with tape. However you do it, allow each thought or feeling to be packaged in some way. Then imagine those thoughts or feelings, in their packages, laid out in front of you. Notice, too, the sense of calmness that goes with having packaged up your thoughts and feelings in this way.
	3	Now, in your mind, look around at those packages and notice which one of them is calling for attention. Sometimes there will be more than one but try to focus on the one that is *most* in need.
	4	Now unpack that one particular issue and allow it some breathing space. Do not immediately put a name to it or rush to 'sort it out'. Instead, allow yourself to immerse yourself in that particular issue.
	5	When you have spent some minutes immersing yourself in this way, ask yourself: 'what is the *feeling* that goes with this issue?'. Do not rush to put a label to it: try one or two labels, tentatively at first. Allow the label to 'emerge' out of the issue. This feeling that emerges in this way can be described as the 'felt sense' of the issue or problem.
	6	Once you have identified this 'felt sense' in this way, allow yourself to explore it for a while. What other feelings go with it? What other thoughts do you associate with it? And so on.

7 Once you have explored the felt sense in this way, ask yourself: what is the *nub of all this*? As you ask this, allow the real issue behind all your thoughts to emerge and to surface. Often, the nub or 'bottom line' is quite different an issue to the one that you started out with.

8 When you have identified the nub or the crux of the issue, allow yourself to explore that a little. Then identify what it is you have to do next. Do not do this too hastily. Again, try out a number of solutions before you settle on what has to be done. Do not rush to make up your mind but rather let the next step emerge of its own accord. Once you have identified the next thing that you have to do acknowledge to yourself that this is the end of the activity for the time being.

9 Allow yourself some more deep breaths. Relax quietly and then rouse yourself gently.

This approach to meditation and problem solving can be very useful when you are under stress and unable to sort out what it is that is worrying you. It is a method of allowing problems and solutions to surface of their own accord rather than one that forces the use of logical or systematic thinking. It is, perhaps, more intuitive than rational. It can also be used as a system for helping *others* to problem-solve.

■ KEEPING A JOURNAL

Another way of exploring the intuitive domain is through keeping a diary or journal. If you structure such a diary through the use of particular headings, you can compare your present 'self' with that of previous weeks or months. One of the problems of diary keeping seems to be that many people start to keep one but few keep it up. Therefore, the more structured you can be the better. The next exercise spells out some useful headings.

Another approach to keeping a journal for the purposes of exploring the intuitive domain is to keep one in which you use 'free writing'. That is to say that every entry starts on a clean page and all you are required to do is to write . . . anything. There are no rules here. You do not have to record anything in particular. All you have to do is write. Almost incidentally, this can be a useful process for developing all sorts of writing skills. If you are required to write essays and papers on a regular basis, this 'free writing' can be a help in developing consistency and style. Some writers make it a discipline to write every day, regardless of whether or not they feel 'inspired'.

When you use the free writing approach, do not stop to edit what you write. The aim is not to produce a polished piece of prose. Keep whatever you write and do not be tempted to tear up pieces that do not read well. As you keep your free writing journal, note how your style changes. Note, too, how the topics of your writing do or do not change. Do you notice constant preoccupations? Do you write about similar or different themes? Are all the themes related in some way?

EXERCISE	**Number 48**
Aim of exercise:	To develop a structure for a self-awareness journal
Activity:	Find a suitable book with lined pages. Use the following headings to record entries in your journal. Try to make daily entries and try to fill in the journal at the same time every day.

- New events
- New knowledge gained
- New skills developed
- Relationship
- Mood
- Thoughts and preoccupations
- Plans and aims
- Other comments

KNOW YOURSELF   Questions about this section

1	I am not sure that I would keep a journal going once I started it	SA	A	U	D	SD
2	I worry about what might happen if someone else read my journal	SA	A	U	D	SD
3	I have kept a journal before . . .	SA	A	U	D	SD

■ KEEPING A RECORD OF YOUR DREAMS

Beliefs about the significance of dreams vary. Some believe that they are of great symbolic significance whilst others believe that they are merely a way of the mind clearing itself out at night. It is interesting to reflect on your own thoughts on the value or otherwise of dreams. One thing is certain: everyone dreams and clearly dreams are a product of your mind. Therefore, they are worth exploring a little. The method suggested here is one adapted from Gestalt therapy. Gestalt is a way of exploring the mind/body through images, thoughts and feelings.

EXERCISE	**Number 49**
Aim of exercise:	To explore your dreams
Activity:	First, keep a 'dream journal'. Keep a notebook by your bed. In the morning, jot down any dream or dream fragment that you can remember. As you get used to doing this it gets easier. At first, you will probably forget to make an entry in the journal and your dream will fade.
	As you keep the journal, notice whether or not there is a pattern to your dreams. Do you dream about the same sorts of things regularly? Do you sometimes have what Jung called a 'big dream' – one that seems to be more vivid or more complex than the others.
	Now for the Gestalt approach to your dreams. Take a dream or a dream fragment and read it through. Then take one particular person or object that appeared in your dream and imagine that you are that person or that object. Now write down a description of yourself as that person or object. You might write as follows:
	'I am David's uncle. I am tall and rather fierce. David doesn't like me particularly . . .' or 'I am a large ocean in Sarah's dream. I am expansive and very cold . . .'
	At first, the process of doing this will feel very odd. As you do it, though, notice the thoughts and feelings that come to you. What do you make of your descriptions? Do they say anything to you about your life situation or your emotions? You may also want to compare what you dream with what has been written about myths and fables [49]. Some people feel that our dreams in some way link us up with a universal heritage or what Jung called 'the collective unconscious' [50]. Certainly, the Aborigines developed this notion in their concept of 'Dreamtime' [51].
	Try writing descriptions, in the first person, of a number of people or objects that appear in a dream or dream fragment. As you get used to the process of writing in this way, you may find that you can abandon the writing part and write the descriptions 'in your head', as you read the dream or dream fragment.
Variations:	If you find that this approach to dream analysis doesn't suit you, merely keep a record of your dreams and note any themes or situations that recur. Then reflect on the degree to which these are indicative of problems or emotional difficulties in your life. Consider how you might resolve these.

Alternatively, you may want to work on your dreams, using the Gestalt approach, working with a friend. In this case, you *verbalise* the description of a person or object in your dream, to this friend. Obviously, you will want to choose a friend that you know well and that you feel comfortable with. It is useful if you work on a reciprocal basis, with each of you taking turns to work with a dream. It is important that you do not try to analyse each others dreams. The theory, here, is that *we* are the best interpreters of our dreams.

KNOW YOURSELF   Questions about this section

1	I feel that dreams are an important means of developing awareness of hidden parts of the self	SA	A	U	D	SD
2	I doubt whether dreams have much to do with waking life	SA	A	U	D	SD
3	I often wonder if other people dream the bizarre dreams that I dream!	SA	A	U	D	SD

■ SUMMARY OF THIS CHAPTER

This chapter has explored intuition or 'knowledge beyond the senses'. It has noted that intuition is a slippery concept. Probably none of the activies in this chapter can *directly* influence how intuitive you are but by focusing on the deeper aspects of yourself and your inner life, the possibility of enhancing your intuitiveness seems likely. Intuition is one of the more underrated aspects of human life. Though, the more you reflect on it, the more it seems likely that we use it all the time. Perhaps it would be even more useful if we paid more attention to it. Specifically, this chapter has explored:

- The nature of intuition
- Synchronicity
- Meditation
- Focusing
- Keeping a journal
- Exploring dreams

7 | The Physical Approach

A healthy person identifies with his body and feels the closeness of his ties to nature.

ALEXANDER LOWEN

Keywords	● Physical status
	● Stress
	● Fitness
	● Health
	● Health For All

Aims of this chapter	● To explore your physical status
	● To identify ways of improving your physical status

■ YOUR PHYSICAL STATUS

You *are* your body. Make no mistakes about that. The temptation is to divorce two parts of you into 'my body' and 'my mind'. Sometimes it is possible to think that some people imagine that their body is just an appendage attached to 'themself'. As we saw in the first chapter, such people talk about their bodies in a detached sort of way: 'I don't like my arms'; 'my body is the wrong shape' and so on. This is more than just a way of talking. It is an indication of the difficulty that people sometimes have in incorporating their body into their sense of self.

Unfortunately, nursing and psychology have sometimes encouraged this split. We study the 'physical aspects of patient care' alongside the 'psychological aspects'. One is taught by physiologists and the other by psychologists and often never the twain meets. In another way, the mind/body split is demonstrated within the profession of nursing by the fact that we have 'general' nurses and 'psychiatric' nurses. A common cliché is to suggest that general nurses take little notice of people's psychological problems and psychiatric nurses know nothing about people's bodies. In this way, we perpetuate the myth that somehow the mind and body can be prised apart.

Part of knowing yourself is knowing your body. Like it or not, the body is as much a subject for scrutiny as any of those more psychological issues discussed in earlier chapters. The next few exercises explore aspects of body awareness.

EXERCISE	**Number 50**
Aim of exercise:	To explore awareness of the body
Activity:	Allow yourself to notice any sensations in your body. Let your attention move from one part of your body to another and notice how each part feels. Are there some parts that are tense while others are relaxed? Does your breathing change as your attention moves its focus? Now allow yourself to *exaggerate* any sensations that you notice. If there is tension, increase it . . . if you are moving your arm or leg slightly, increase that movement. Now notice how you can take responsibility for how your body feels and that you can *choose* to relax or tense many aspects of your body. Notice those parts of the body that are fairly constantly tense. Now reverse the procedure. Pay attention to those parts of the body in which you exaggerated a sensation and try to reverse the procedure. Thus, try to relax those parts that are tense. Stop any movement in your arms or legs. Notice what happens as you allow yourself to stop.

EXERCISE	**Number 51**
Aim of exercise:	To explore your physical movements in everyday life
Activity:	Choose a fairly mundane activity such as cleaning your teeth or opening an envelope. First, carry out the activity at normal speed and *notice* how you do it. Notice the amount of energy that you put into the activity and notice what muscle clusters are involved. Then, slow the activity to about half speed and notice what happens. Then try the activity again, using less effort to carry out the task. Allow yourself to notice yourself 'in action' on frequent occasions throughout the day and practice reducing the effort taken to complete various tasks. Notice when everyday tasks seem to take more effort and when they are easy to carry out. Make a note of how you are feeling when these changes occur.

EXERCISE	**Number 52**
Aim of exercise:	To explore your attractiveness
Activity:	Write down on a sheet of paper, the qualities that you associate with a physically attractive person. Try to write quickly and write in short, descriptive paragraphs. Now ask yourself the following questions:

- What makes those qualities attractive?
- How did you develop this sense of 'attractiveness'?
- Would other people share your view?
- In terms of your description, how attractive are you?

Our culture places a high premium on good looks. Have you been socialised into accepting that idea or do you feel that other human qualities are equally, if not more, important?

EXERCISE	**Number 53**
Aim of exercise:	Exploring your concepts of sexuality
Activity:	This is a curious exercise! Imagine that you are a member of the opposite sex. What sort of person would you be? What would you *look* like? Have you ever wished that you were a member of the opposite sex?.

KNOW YOURSELF   Questions about this section

1	I do not like my body very much	SA	A	U	D	SD
2	My body tends to reflect my personality	SA	A	U	D	SD
3	I find discussion about bodies slightly embarrassing	SA	A	U	D	SD

■ MAINTAINING PHYSICAL HEALTH

Nursing is a fairly physical activity. It is also concerned with health. It is noticeable how the emphasis in nursing has shifted over the last few years from *illness* to *health* and wellness. It is appropriate, then, for us to monitor our own health. There are numerous reasons for this. A few would be:

- In order that we stay healthy ourselves
- So that we act as role models for colleagues
- So that we act as role models for patients
- In order to maintain psychological wellbeing

Woodcock and Francis [52] offer the following principles for maintaining physical health:

- *Watch your weight.* All nurses appreciate the dangers on the cardiovascular of excess weight. It seems sensible to moderate your diet and if necessary consider cutting down on certain foods, in a planned and reasonable way.
- Take some exercise that you enjoy. Running, squash, jogging and swimming have become particularly popular sports. The point is, though, to *enjoy* how you exercise and to do it regularly.
- *Balance your life activities.* Everyone gets dull if they do the same things over and over. Try to balance physical, intellectual and social activities. It is easy to become a 'sport bore' if your whole life revolves around keeping and getting fit. On the other hand, you will not feel very healthy if you *never* exercise.
- *Beware of unhealthy habits.* The two obvious ones, here, are smoking and excessive drinking. All nurses are aware of the dangers of smoking and it has become increasingly unfashionable to smoke. Many people find it difficult to give up. Macleod-Clark, Kendal and Haverty [53] suggest that in planning how to help someone give up smoking the smoker needs to be assessed in terms of:
  (a) motivation to give up,
  (b) health beliefs and worries about smoking,
  (c) level of knowledge about smoking and health,
  (d) Factors influencing smoking behaviour, e.g. family circumstances,
  (e) Factual information, e.g. numbers smoked per day.

The Health Education Council [54] suggest a 10 point plan of action for getting fit:

1   GET MOVING – choose activities you really enjoy
2   Make it regular – preferably three times a week
3   Keep it up for at least 15 minutes a time
4   Start gently and increase the effort gradually
5   Get family or friends to join you
6   Keep a watch on your weight – stay slim
7   Cut down on fatty foods – especially dairy products and meat
8   Steady on the sugar and sweet things
9   Eat more fibre – like brown or wholemeal bread, fruit, cereals and potatoes
10   GET STARTED – NOW!

When planning a fitness campaign, it is important to bear in mind the factors about exercise that affect fitness. They can be identified as follows:

- *Type of exercise*: the form of exercise that you choose is important. Clearly, hard cycling is more strenuous than gentle walking.
- *Exercise intensity*: how hard you exercise affects your pulse rate. That rate is affected by two things: (a) *exercise rate*: how fast you exercise, and (b) *exercise load*: the resistance against which you exercise (e.g. whether or not you run up steep hills or pedal hard in a high gear on a bike).
- *Exercise duration*: how long you exercise affects your pulse rate. General fitness is best improved by increasing duration of exercise rather than intensity.
- *Exercise frequency*: how often you exercise is also important. It does not affect your exercise pulse rate directly but it affects the rate of improvement of fitness.

A word of caution is in order here. If you are ill, receiving medical treatment or are over 35, it is wise to consult your GP before commencing a new exercise programme.

EXERCISE	**Number 54**
Aim of exercise:	To reflect on your own physical health
Activity:	Using the following grid, identify the factors that support your being healthy and those that work against it. Put a tick against any of the factors that apply to you and reflect on whether or not you have more positive factors than negative ones.

Positive Factors	Tick if this applies	Negative Factors	Tick if this applies
I take regular exercise		I rarely exercise	
I eat healthily		I tend to eat a lot of 'junk' food	
I balance work with social events		I tend to be something of a 'workaholic'	
I am not overweight		I am overweight	
I relax easily		I am tense a lot of the time	
I organise what I have to do		I deal with things as they crop up	
I feel healthy		I do not feel healthy	
My health is important to me		I rarely think about my health	
I drink moderately or not at all		I smoke	

■ COPING WITH STRESS

Nursing is often described as a stressful occupation. What is stress? Bailey and Clarke [55] identify three approaches to it:

1   Stress can be defined as something outside the person which he reacts to. In this model, for example, bad lighting or disturbing life events can be examples of stress: the person *responds* to that stress by experiencing *strain*. The problem with this approach can be that it tends to treat the person as a passive respondent to stress. Bailey and Clarke call this the *stimulus based model*.

2   Almost the opposite approach to the stimulus based model is the *response based model*. Here, stress is used to denote a person's physiological response to a difficult environment or distressing

life event. Perhaps the best known example of this approach is Hans Selye's General Adaptation Syndrome [56]. He defines the stress syndrome as follows:

The non-specific response of the body to any demand made upon it.

Stress, for Selye, causes physiological changes in the body and a whole range of stressors can cause similar sorts of physiological responses.

3   The mid position between these two is the *transactional model of stress*. This model acknowledges that an individual's *perception* of a situation plays a large part in determining whether or not that situation is stressful. This model takes into account the fact that different people find different situations stressful at different points in their lives. The person in this model is neither a passive recipient of stress nor a consistent responder to it. Instead, the person responds to difficult life events via his or her idiosyncratic *coping style*. This approach is more of a *psychological* one than the two previous ones.

The first two of these approaches to stress tend to favour a physiological view of stress. Stressful events occur and the body responds accordingly. The last approach, the more psychological, acknowledges that individuals respond differently to a variety of stimuli. What causes a stress response in one person may spur another on. Arguably, it is difficult to lay down 'typical' stress responses: everything, it would seem is dependent upon *this* individual's history, his expectations, his physical and psychological status and his previous experience. The approach taken here is that what is important is for you to identify YOUR ways of coping and YOUR ways of dealing with stress. By becoming more self-aware it is possible to notice your reactions and to choose what you do about them. That choice is broadened by having knowledge of a range of possible ways of coping.

EXERCISE	**Number 55**
Aim of exercise:	To identify your stressors
Activity:	This is an activity developed from Meg Bond's work [57]. On a large sheet of paper, write down the following headings, spaced out on the sheet:

  1   Things that cause me stress from within myself
  2   Things other people do that cause me stress
  3   Factors in the world-at-large that cause me stress

Then 'brainstorm' your own reactions to the three headings. Under each heading write down as many factors as you can think of. Examples of each may include:

Things that cause me stress from within myself:
(a) the way I feel about myself
(b) my shyness
(c) my anger . . .

Things other people do that cause me stress:
(a) run my life for me!
(b) order me about at work
(c) fall out of love with me . . .

Factors in the world-at-large that cause me stress:
(a) cruelty to animals
(b) people starving
(c) apartheid . . .

Variations:	It is very useful to do this activity in a group and to compare the sorts of things that stress each of you.

EXERCISE	**Number 56**
Aim of exercise:	To examine the ways that you cope with stress
Activity:	In the box below, is a list of ways of coping with stress. Read through it and in the first column, put a tick against those methods that you frequently use to cope with stress. In the second column, use a symbol according to the following code:

A   Need to consider using this method
B   Never heard of the method and need to find out more
C   A negative method of coping with stress
D   Not my sort of method

Then examine your list and notice any trends that emerge as to the ways you cope with stress. Many people tend to go through life putting up with things, rather than confronting them. Stress is one of those things. Consider whether or not you are doing enough to combat stress in your life and whether or not you are using a variety of methods to combat it.

Methods of coping with stress	I frequently use this method	A, B, C or D
Ignore it		
Keep a journal and 'write it all out'		
Talk about it to friends		
Use relaxation methods		
Meditate		
Take part in sports and exercise		
Have diverting hobbies		
Smoke a lot		
Get angry		
Use martial arts		
Use co-counselling		
Drink excessively		
Get someone to give me a massage		
Cry		
Become aggressive with other people		
Get tense		
Play music		
Write poetry, music, stories		
Pray		
Use Yoga		
Use biofeedback		
Drive very fast		
Nothing . . .		
Use other methods		

EXERCISE	**Number 57**
Aim of exercise:	To experience complete relaxation
Activity:	Lie on your back with your hands by your sides . . . stretch your legs out and have your feet about a foot apart . . . pay attention to your breathing . . . take two or three deep breaths and feel yourself begin to relax . . . now let your breathing become gentle, slow and relaxed . . . now allow your head sink into the floor . . . your head is sinking and you feel more and more relaxed . . . allow your forehead to become smooth and relaxed . . . allow your cheeks and the rest of your face to relax . . . let your jaw relax and feel the tension easing in your temples . . . let yourself relax more and more . . . let your neck . . . and your shoulders relax . . . now become aware of your right arm . . . let your right arm relax . . . your upper right arm . . . your lower right arm and now your right hand . . . the whole of your right arm and hand . . . completely relaxed . . . now become aware of your left arm . . . let your left arm relax . . . your upper left arm . . . your lower left arm and now your left hand . . . the whole of your left arm and hand completely relaxed . . . now allow your chest and trunk to feel heavy and relaxed . . . now your hips and pelvis and feel your seat sinking into the floor . . . now put your attention into your right leg . . . feel your right leg becoming heavy and relaxed . . . now your right foot . . . allow it to feel very heavy and very relaxed . . . now put your attention into your left leg . . . feel your left leg becoming heavy and relaxed . . . now your left foot . . . allow it to feel very heavy and very relaxed. Now notice how relaxed you feel and allow yourself a few minutes complete relaxation before you slowly sit and then stand up.

Notice the difference between how you feel *before* you do this activity and how you feel after. Notice if any particular sets of muscles tend to get tense. Notice, too, *when* you tend to get tense and notice in what particular nursing situations you get tense.

Variations:	1	This script can be talked through to a group or can be dictated onto a tape for use by the individual. There is much to be said for the take being prepared by the person who is going to use the tape so that they get used to hearing their own voice suggesting they relax. In this way, the injunction to relax becomes self-reinforcing.
	2	The script can be memorised and used as a means of relaxation whenever you need to use it.

KNOW YOURSELF	**Questions about this section**					
1	I cope with stress fairly well	SA	A	U	D	SD
2	I would like to use other methods of dealing with stress	SA	A	U	D	SD
3	Other people seem to cope with stress better than I do	SA	A	U	D	SD

■ TAKING A GLOBAL VIEW: HEALTH PROMOTION

All of us as nurses have responsibility for other people's, as well as our own health. Helping people to take responsibility for their health needs through education and practical help is part of the expanding role of the nurse. Ashton and Seymour [58] define the following five principles of health promotion:

1 Health promotion actively involves the population in the setting of everyday life rather than focusing on people who are at risk for specific conditions and in contact with medical services.
2 Health promotion is directed towards action on the causes of ill-health.
3 Health promotion uses many different approaches which combine to improve health. These include education and information, community developments and organisation, health advocacy and legislation.
4 Health promotion depends particularly on public participation.
5 Health professionals − especially those in primary health care − have an important part to play in nurturing health promotion and enabling it to take place.

In 1981 the 34th World Health Assembly accepted as WHO policy that organisation's publication *Global Strategy of Health For All by the Year 2000* [59]. According to this policy, the task ahead is to make sure that by the year 2000:

> . . . all people in all countries should have at least such a level of health that they are capable of working productively and of participating actively in the social life of the community in which they live.

Appendix III of this book identifies the focus of targets for 'Health for All' by the year 2000 in Europe, published in 1985. This, then, is the larger health canvas, beyond individual self-awareness. Given the recent changes in Europe it is interesting to ponder on the degree to which such health care options can be and/or have been realised.

EXERCISE	Number 58
Aim of exercise:	To explore your reactions to 'Health for All'
Activity:	Read through the target statements in Appendix three. Consider the part that *you* play in this process of health promotion. Consider, also, the part you play *locally* in health promotion, as a role model, giver of information and health care professional. Think about what you need to do to enhance your ability as a promoter of health.

■ SUMMARY OF THIS CHAPTER

This chapter has been about physical health. It has acknowledged that you *are* your body and that it is artificial to make a distinction between the mind and body. Specifically, the chapter has considered:

- Your physical status
- Maintaining your health
- Coping with stress
- The global view
- Health promotion

8 | The Self and Others

Keywords	• Relationships
	• Groups
	• Facilitation
	• Listening
	• Responding
	• Questions
	• Reflection
	• Empathy development
	• Negotiation

Aims of this chapter	• To explore your relationships with others
	• To examine ways of enhancing your relationships
	• To explore skills of relating to others

None of us lives alone. We all live and work with other people. The whole point of becoming more self-aware is not to help us in isolation but to help in our relationships with others. Part of the process of developing self-awareness is the process of exploring our relationships with others. More than this, we *need* other people. We need them for nurturance and encouragement; we need them to help and teach us; we need them to help us set limits on ourselves. Without others, we would neither know who we were nor would be able to monitor our behaviour. Other people are telling us who we are.

■ RELATING TO PATIENTS

First, how well do you relate to patients? Is the whole business of getting on with them easy or do you have to struggle to relate and talk to them? No doubt you have undergone some training in interpersonal skills but different people react differently to such training. Some people feel that it is always best to be 'natural', whilst others feel that detailed training is essential for everyone in the caring professions. The problem, here, is this: what do we mean by 'natural'? Often we mean that we are being natural when we do not have to think about what we do or say. This is a flawed description. Even if we do not *now* have to think about what we do or say, presumably we *learned* all this behaviour at some time. Presumably you are not just *born* the way you become as an adult!

If you did learn to be who you are now, you are capable of unlearning some aspects of it. This is the optimistic fact about human relationships. Whether we like being 'natural' or not, we can always improve the way we relate to others by paying attention to our relationships.

EXERCISE	**Number 59**
Aim of exercise:	To explore your relationships with patients
Activity:	Read through the list below and rate yourself using one of the following codes:

1 I enjoy relating with this sort of person and do so easily
2 I am reasonably confident relating to this sort of person
3 I am not sure how well I relate to this sort of person
4 I find relating to this sort of person difficult
5 I do not like relating to this sort of person

The types of people	Your rating (1–5)
A middle aged man on a medical ward	
A 16 year old boy on an adolescent unit	
An elderly woman on a care of the elderly ward	
A gay person	
A girl or woman of your own age	
A psychiatric patient	

The types of people	Your rating (1–5)
A person who is dying	
A person from a different social class to yours	
An older person with a different skin colour to yours	

Now consider the following questions:

- How difficult was this exercise?
- Where you surprised at any of your responses?
- What *makes* the people you have difficulty with difficult?
- How *like you* are the people that you have difficulty with?

KNOW YOURSELF!   Questions about this section

1   I relate to all patients impartially and treat them all the same   SA   A   U   D   SD

2   It is unprofessional to treat some people differently   SA   A   U   D   SD

3   I find *some* people very difficult to get on with   SA   A   U   D   SD

▮ RELATING TO COLLEAGUES

We work in teams. None of us offers care independently of others. All sorts of rivalries and professional differences of opinion can crop up in relationships with our colleagues. Apart from those, it seems reasonable to suppose that we will always get on better with some sorts of people than with others. The next exercise helps you to consider your relationships with the people that you work with.

EXERCISE	**Number 60**
Aim of exercise:	To explore your relationships with your colleagues
Activity:	Read through the list below and rate yourself using one of the following codes:
1	I enjoy relating with this sort of person and do so easily

2 I am reasonably confident relating to this sort of person
3 I am not sure how well I relate to this sort of person
4 I find relating to this sort of person difficult
5 I do not like relating to this sort of person

The types of people	Your rating (1–5)
A person who is in charge of the place in which I am working	
A person who is junior to me	
People who are in my learning group	
Tutors or lecturers	
Anyone 'in charge'	
Intense people	
Overly relaxed people	
People who are particularly knowledgeable or skilful	
People other than nurses	

Now consider the following questions:

- How do your relationships with your colleages compare with your relationships with people you worked with in previous jobs? Do you still like and dislike the same sorts of people?
- How like *you* are the people that you don't get on with so well?
- What are *you* like in positions of authority?
- How important is it to get on with your colleagues?

■ BLOCKS IN COMMUNICATION

Living alongside others is not always easy. Some of the factors which make co-existence with others difficult are these:

- Lack of clear communication
- People's difficulty in expressing what they mean
- Prejudice
- Faulty expectations of others
- Lack of self-confidence

- Lack of assertiveness
- Pressure of work
- Environmental problems
- Continued close proximity to others
- Invasion of privacy

KNOW YOURSELF!   **Questions about this section**

---

1   I will learn from the people   SA   A   U   D   SD
I dislike and will not make the
same mistakes as them

---

2   The people I do not get on   SA   A   U   D   SD
with are probably quite like me

---

3   I accept that it is impossible to   SA   A   U   D   SD
get on with everybody that
you work with

■ GROUPS

We all live and work in groups. Sometimes we are called upon to organise and run groups. Consider, for example, the following groups:

- Ward meetings
- Case conferences
- Planning teams
- Relatives meetings
- Learning groups
- Therapy groups
- Stress management groups
- Primary nursing groups

Depending on the sort of nursing you have chosen, it is likely that you will be asked to facilitate one or more of the above groups at some time. To do this involves *facilitation skills* or skills in planning, organising and maintaining the smooth running of the group. Heron [60] offers a useful six-point framework for organising and running groups that he calls Dimensions or Facilitator Style. The six dimensions are:

- The planning dimension
- The meaning dimension
- The confronting dimension
- The feeling dimension
- The structuring dimension
- The valuing dimension

The six dimensions of facilitator style can be used to make decisions about how *this* group is run at *this* time. Not all of the dimensions will be used in every group. Decisions about which dimension will be used during which group will depend on the type of group that is being run, the aims of the group, your own personality and the needs of the participants.

The dimensions cover most aspects of the setting up and running of groups. What follows is an adaptation of Heron's model.

The Planning Dimension

This dimension is concerned with the setting up of the group. Group members always need to know *why* they are in a particular group. Therefore the group facilitator needs to make certain decisions about how to identify the aims and objectives of the group. She has at least three options here:

- She can decide upon the aims and objectives herself, before setting up the group at all.
- She can negotiate the aims and objectives with the group. In this case, she will decide on some of those aims and objectives. The group will decide on others.
- She can encourage the group to set its own aims and objectives. In this case, all the facilitator does is to turn up on a certain day with a 'title' or name for the group. All further decisions about what the group is to achieve are made by the group.

The first example, above, illustrates the traditional learning group approach. The nurse educator (for example) who uses this approach, will have set aims and objectives for a particular lesson, that she has planned in advance.

The second example illustrates the negotiated group approach. The nurse working as a group therapist (for example), will meet the group for the first time and work with them to identify what that group can achieve in the time that they meet together.

The third example illustrates the fully client-centred or student-centred approach to working with groups. Here, the nurse does not anticipate the needs or wants of the group at all. Instead, she allows the learning, therapy or discussion group to set its own agenda. Such an approach needs careful handling if it is not to degenerate into an aimless series of meetings.

Other aspects of the planning dimension include making decisions about the following issues:

- The number of group participants.
- Whether or not particular 'rules' will apply to the group,
- Whether or not group membership will remain the same throughout the life of the group (the closed group) or whether new members will be allowed to join (the open group).

Again, such planning decisions can be taken either unilaterally by the facilitator or via negotiation with the group.

The Meaning Dimension

We all need to know *why* we are in a group. This aspect of group facilitation is concerned with what sense group members make of being in the group. As with the previous dimension, at least three options are open here:

- The nurse as facilitator can offer explanations, theories or models to enable group members to make sense of what is happening. Thus a nurse running a support group for bereaved relatives may offer a theoretical model of bereavement to enable those relatives to have a framework for understanding what is happening to them.
- The nurse as facilitator may sometimes offer 'interpretations' of what is going on. At other times, she will listen to group members' perceptions of what is happening. This may frequently happen in any open discussion group or a case conference.
- The facilitator offers no explanations or theories but encourages group members to verbalise their own ideas, thoughts and theories. This is the non-directive mode of working with meaning in a group.

The Confronting Dimension

When people work together, all sorts of conflicts can arise. Sometimes these conflicts are overt and show themselves in arguments and disagreements. Sometimes, a 'hidden agenda' is at work. Conflicts sit just beneath the surface of group life. Whilst they affect it in various ways, they cannot be worked with unless the group addresses them directly. The confronting dimension of facilitation is concerned with ways in which individual members and the group-as-a-whole are challenged. The three ways of working in this dimension are as follows:

- The nurse can challenge the group or its members directly. Thus, she asks questions, makes suggestions, offers interpretations of behaviour in the group. Her aim is to encourage the group and its members to confront what is happening at various levels.
- The nurse can facilitate an atmosphere in which people feel safe enough to challenge each other (and the facilitator). In help in this process, the following 'ground rules' for direct and clear communication can help:
  (a) Say 'I' rather than 'you', 'we' or 'people' when discussing issues in the group.
  (b) Speak directly to other people, rather than about them. Thus 'I am angry with you, David' is better than 'I am angry with people in this group'.
- The nurse can choose not to confront at all. In this case, two

things may happen a) no confrontation takes place and the group gets 'stuck', or b) the group learns to challenge itself, without assistance from the facilitator.

The first example of confrontation, above, is the traditional 'chairperson' mode of facilitation. The nurse who uses this approach, stays in control of the group. The negotiated style of confrontation is one that can be used in discussion groups and informal teaching sessions. The third example is one that can be used in meetings and discussion that are of a very formal kind. If it is used in therapy and self-awareness groups, the chances are that the 'hidden agenda' will not get addressed or that the group members will outgrow the need for the facilitator. It is arguable that *all* groups should aim at becoming independent of the group leader.

The Feeling Dimension

Therapy groups, self-awareness groups and certain sorts of learning groups, tend to generate emotion in participants. The feeling dimension is concerned with how such emotional expression is dealt with. Decisions that can be made in this domain include the following:

- Will emotional release be *encouraged*? This may be appropriate in a therapy or social skills training group.
- Is there to be an explicit *contract* with the group about emotional release? Here, the nurse may suggest at the beginning of the first group meeting that emotional release is 'allowed', thus giving group members permission ot express emotions.
- Does the nurse feel skilled in handling emotional release? If not, she may want to develop skills in coping with other people's feelings, especially when these involve the overt expression of tears, anger or fear. Training in cathartic work is needed here.

The Structuring Dimension

Structure is part of the way we live. It is a necessary part of group life. Without it, the group can fall apart. The issue, here, is *how* such structure is developed. Again, at least three options open up in this domain.

- The nurse can decide on the total structure of the group. In a social skills group, for example, she may introduce a variety of exercises and activities that allow participants to learn how to answer the telephone, introduce themselves at parties or take faulty goods back to a shop. At all times, she remains in control of the overall structure.
- The nurse can encourage group members to organise certain

aspects of the life and structure of the group. Thus the ward sister who is running a learning group may invite students to read and discuss seminar papers. In this respect, she is handing over some of the structure to group members.

- The nurse can play a minimal role in structuring the life of the group. The extreme example of this is the 'Tavistock' approach to group therapy in which the group starts and finishes at particular times. Between those times the facilitator makes no attempt to 'lead' the group. This is not for the uninitiated!

As a general rule it is probably better for the new facilitator to start with lots of structure (which is imposed by her). As she gains confidence in running groups, she can gradually hand over some of that structure to group members.

The Valuing Dimension

Do you enjoy being in a group? This aspect of group facilitation is concerned with creating a supportive and valuing atmosphere in which the group can work. No group will succeed if the atmosphere is one of distrust and suspicion. The issues, here, are the following:

- Is the facilitator confident enough to allow disagreement, discussion and varieties of points of view?
- Does she have sufficient self-awareness to know the effect that she is having on the group?
- Is she skilled, positive, life asserting and encouraging?

Learning to value other people (and oneself) comes with experience of running groups, developing a range of therapeutic skills such as counselling, social skills and assertiveness.

What has been described here is a structured way of exploring how groups are organised and run. There are other ways of thinking about groups but this one is fairly straightforward to learn and seems to cover most aspects of the planning and facilitation of a variety of group activities.

EXERCISE	Number 61
Aim of exercise:	Noticing the facilitation style of others
Activity:	Try to memorise the six dimensions of facilitator styles. Next time you are in a group, observe the facilitator (or group leader) closely and notice which aspects of the six he or she uses most effectively. Notice, too, if there are any of the dimensions that are *not* evident.

Variations:	You may want to try using the dimensions, consciously, in a group. For this, you need to work with a small group of colleagues or friends, say about six in all. Then you practise using the dimensions for a period of about half an hour. At the end of that period, you disclose to the group how you think you did. Then, you ask them to tell you how *they* think you did. After you have had half an hour of trying out various styles, someone else can have a go. This is a useful way of building up a repertoire of group skills in a supportive atmosphere.
	After you have practised in this way, try out your skills in a 'real' group: in the clinical or educational setting.

KNOW YOURSELF!   Questions about this section

1	I do not feel ready to run groups yet	SA	A	U	D	SD
2	Nurses tend not to get specific education and training in running groups	SA	A	U	D	SD
3	Some people are good in groups whilst others are not; you cannot *train* yourself to be a group leader	SA	A	U	D	SD

■ INTERPERSONAL SKILLS

One necessity in working with others is that we demonstrate a reasonable level of interpersonal competence. In this section, we explore aspects of interpersonal skills that are useful in both our dealings with patients and our working with colleagues.

Listening and Responding

Listening is probably the most caring act of all. Often, though, we only give *half* our attention to another person. Often, we are distracted by our own thoughts or by rehearsing what we are going to say to the other person in return. Some people, too, are 'sentence finishers'. They anticipate what the other person is trying to say and put words into their mouths. This is unlikely to be very helpful and certainly is not very sociable. The next exercise asks you to explore your own listening and responding style.

EXERCISE	**Number 62**

Aim of exercise:	To explore your listening and responding style

Activity:	Next time you have a conversation with someone, consciously notice the following things:

- How you stand or sit in relation to the other person.
- Whether or not you maintain easy eye contact with them.
- What 'minimal prompts' you use ('mm's, head nods, 'yes's').
- Whether or not you get impatient with the other person as they talk.
- Whether or not you really *listen* to them (this will be particularly difficult, as you are now being asked to *monitor* your listening: this, itself, will be slightly distracting!).
- Your facial expression as you listen.
- How often, and the manner in which, you respond.
- How much talking *you* do and how much you allow the other person to talk.
- Whether or not you relate everything that the other person says to *your* experience (e.g. 'I know what you mean . . . I'm just like that myself . . .'). Too much of this self-reference can not only be irritating but it does not allow the other person to really talk about what is on their mind.

This is quite a list! You may not be able to observe all of these items in one sitting. Instead, just become more and more aware of your listening and responding behaviours. Notice the difference between listening and responding to a patient in a clinical setting and listening and responding with a group of friends in a pub or other social setting. What differences are there?

Basic Responding Skills

There are many situations in which we are called upon to listen and respond to others, therapeutically. A therapeutic conversation is slightly different to other sorts in that the *focus* of it is not oneself but the other person. In everyday conversations, the focus fluctuates fairly freely between one person and the other. In a therapeutic conversation, the aim is to help the other person to talk a problem through, to express how they feel, to identify some goals. A short list of responding skills includes:

- Asking open questions
- Asking closed questions
- Reflecting feelings
- Reflecting content
- Checking for understanding
- Developing empathy

Asking Open Questions

Open questions usually begin with How?, Why?, What? or Where? They are questions to which you cannot easily anticipate the answer. They allow the talker to expand on what they are saying and how they are feeling. Examples of open questions are:

- How are you feeling at the moment?
- Why did you go there?
- What happened when you did that?
- Where do you feel uncomfortable?

Whilst open questions are particularly useful for helping people to develop their thoughts, be careful of asking too many 'Why?' questions. They can tend to sound both interrogative and a bit moralistic. They can also make it sound as though you are blaming the other person in some way. For a more detailed discussion on the problems with 'Why?' questions, see some of the books that have been written about counselling and interpersonal skills [61].

Closed Questions

These are useful for obtaining specific information. They are questions that usually elicit a short, often one word answer. Very often you can anticipate the sort of answer you are likely to get with a closed question. Examples include:

- Did you say that you had two children?
- What is your son's name?
- What number do you live at?
- What is your middle name?

Too many closed questions tend to spoil a conversation. Whilst they can be useful when you need to know an important detail, they are less versatile than open questions.

Reflecting Feelings

Here, the aim is to reflect back to the talker something of what that person is *feeling*. Reflections of this sort help the other person to identify and clarify their feelings. Go easy on these, though: too many tend to sound a little parrot-like! An example of a reflection of feeling is as follows:

'I've felt uncomfortable since I came into hospital. Partly its the operation. Some of its to do with being away from home...'

'Your feeling generally uncomfortable at the moment...'

'Upset as well. I can face the operation. Its the way I feel that's difficult...'

Reflecting Content

This sort of reflection is of a more concrete nature. Here, the actual words used by the other person are reflected back to encourage them to say more.

> 'I used to go to the community centre. It's changed down there, though. You used to be able to talk to people. Now they haven't got time for you...'

> 'They haven't got time...'

> 'They *want* to talk to you, I suppose. It's just that they're so busy, they always have so many people there. I can talk to my GP easier...'

> 'You can talk to your GP...'

> 'He's known me for years. He's always had time for me. And you can't say that about *most* GPs...'

Again, reflection of content needs to be used judiciously. Many people have heard of the technique and many people have learned to use it on counselling and inter-personal skills courses. It is useful when it is used well and noticeable when it is used badly!

Checking for Understanding

This can mean two things. First, you do not understand quite what the other person is saying, so you check with them:

> 'I'm sorry, I missed the first bit of what you said...'

The second is where you summarise what the other person has said in order to see that you have got it right.

> '...so you are saying that you feel mixed up about whether or not to stay in nursing but you're not sure you want to discuss it at the moment with your tutor?...'

Developing Empathy

Here, you demonstrate that you are understanding and empathising with the other person. Usually, empathy developing statements are tentative ones:

> '...it sounds as though you are pretty angry at the moment...'

> '...it feels like you've had these feelings bottled up for a long time...'

Empathy building statements can be helpful in conveying that you are 'with' the other person. Again, like reflection, they should be used sparingly. Used 'automatically' they can sound very contrived and artificial: the very things that you don't want to convey!

EXERCISE	**Number 63**
Aim of exercise:	To explore other people's skills
Activity:	Next time that you are with someone that you feel has good counselling or interpersonal skills, listen to what they say. More than that, listen to *how* they say what they say. Listen out for examples of the skills identified above:

- Open questions
- Closed questions
- Reflecting feelings
- Reflecting content
- Checking for understanding
- Developing empathy

EXERCISE	**Number 64**
Aim of exercise:	To develop your own responding skills
Activity:	Now you are being *asked* to be artificial and contrived! Next time you are talking things through with someone, make a real effort to include at least TWO of the following in your conversation:

- Open questions
- Closed questions
- Reflecting feelings
- Reflecting content
- Checking for understanding
- Developing empathy

Variations:	Try to monitor and vary the responses you use when talking to others. Although this particular exercise is quite difficult because you are being asked to notice and change what you say to others, it is an important part of learning the skills of therapeutic conversation. After a while, the skills become a natural part of your repertoire. After all, many people use these interventions as a matter of course. It is *concentrating* on using them that makes them difficult. On the other hand, if you never try to use them, you will never learn how to.

1	Conversations should be natural; you do not need to learn to talk to other people	SA	A	U	D	SD
2	Nurses, as a rule, are not particularly good at helping people to talk through their problems	SA	A	U	D	SD
3	I am generally quite a good listener	SA	A	U	D	SD

■ NEGOTIATING

We have to negotiate all the time. Consider the following situations:

- Changing your days off
- Deciding on what you learn in a block of training or on a study day
- Deciding on where you go, when you go out with a friend
- Trying to work out your finances with your bank manager

All of these situations call for negotiation skills. Many of the skills described in other parts of this book come into play here: assertiveness, relationship, facilitation and decision making skills. In negotiation, however, there are some particular problems. Prior to negotiation, two or more people have interests in the outcome of a discussion. Kennedy [62] identifies a variety of criteria for successful negotiation. Amongst the items on his check list are:

- Do not state a grievance, negotiate a remedy,
- Good negotiators face the same dilemmas as everybody else. (This is particularly important. It is easy to imagine that the person that you are negotiating with always has the upper hand.)
- Negotiating involves both sides in a voluntary consent to a joint decision.
- The written word has greater authority than the spoken word.

EXERCISE	**Number 65**
Aim of exercise:	To explore your negotiation skills
Activity:	Consider the following situations and then rate yourself

against each of them in terms of how skilled you feel you are in handling the negotiation. Consider, then, what you need to do to gain the skills in those situations in which you feel weakest.

In the left hand column, put one of the following letters:

A   I could negotiate easily in this situation
B   I am not sure that I could negotiate in this situation
C   I could not negotiate in this situation

Situation	Rating
A lecturer in the college of nursing asks you what you need to study in a revision block. You know that you are weak in physiology but you know that your colleagues do not want to study it any further.	
You are asked by a senior nurse to start a relatives' support group and that once you have, you will be able to go on a training course in group facilitation. You do not feel confident enough to start the group but you also want to go on the course.	
You are renting a flat in an area of the town that you like. You know that property is scarce in that area. Your landlord tells you that your rent is to be increased substantially to help cover the cost of repairs.	
You return a jersey that you have bought to the shop where you bought it. You have found it to have a small rip under one of the arms. The manager of the shop says that you can have a credit note for the goods. You want your money back.	
You are asked to talk to a group of students at a large conference run by a large company. The conference organiser says that he will pay your train fare to the conference but regrets that he cannot pay you a fee.	

Variations

Observe negotiators that you identify as being skilful and notice what they do and say. Notice, also, negotiations that take place in public, on television. Observe the degree to which timing, use of language, non-verbal communication and being clear all play their part in negotiations [63]. Compare the skills of negotiation with other sorts of relationship skills identified and discussed in this book.

KNOW YOURSELF **Questions about this section**

1	I would rather leave negotiations to other people	SA	A	U	D	SD
2	I believe that you have to know your own limits and know when to back off	SA	A	U	D	SD
3	Negotiating is not very dignified	SA	A	U	D	SD

■ SUMMARY OF THIS CHAPTER

This chapter has explored your relationships with other people. It has suggested that there are a variety of things that you can do to enhance the likelihood of your conversations with patients being therapeutic. It has discussed:

- Relating to patients
- Relating to colleagues
- Blocks in communication
- Group facilitation
- Interpersonal skills
- Listening and responding
- Basic responding skills
- Negotiation

9 | Self-Presentation

We are what we pretend to be. So be careful what *you pretend to be*

KURT VONNEGUT

A man may have a resounding title, a great position of authority, money, influence, but if we notice that his hands are constantly fidgeting on his desk, that he can't look us in the eye, that he crosses and uncrosses his legs as if suffering from a bad itch in the crotch and that when the phone rings, he can't make up his mind whether or not to pick it up or ignore it, we can then, I think, safely conclude that he is not a man of power.

MICHAEL KORDA

Keywords	● Curriculum vitae
	● Appearance
	● Introductions
	● Telephone skills
	● Emotions
	● Assertion
	● Personal skills

Aims of this chapter	● To help you write a curriculum vitae
	● To explore your perception of your appearance
	● To examine your communication skills
	● Audit your personal skills

All through this book you have explored who you are. In this chapter we turn to how you present yourself to other people. All of us, as nurses, are constantly on show. It is no use us just feeling good about ourselves. We must do more than that. We must learn to present ourselves to others in a good light. This does not arise out of vanity or a misplaced sense of showmanship. It is part of what it means to respect and to care for others. If we want to help others we must look the part as well as feel the part. Also, if our careers are to develop, we need to make the best presentation of self as possible. Like it or not, people notice what we look like.

■ SELF-PREPARATION 1: THE CV

Your curriculum vitae, or 'life curriculum', is often your first point of contact with another person when you are communicating through the post. It is important that your CV 'sells' you. If you produce a hurried and scruffy CV you cannot hope to impress the person that you are writing to.

A CV lists your achievements to date. People often wonder what sorts of things should and should not go in one. The following is a list of the sorts of things that are suitable for inclusion. In the exercise that follows, we explore how to lay out and develop your own CV:

- Your full name
- Your full address
- Your date of birth
- Your current job
- A brief description of your current job
- The history of your education to date
- The history of your work to date
- A list of special skills that you have
- Club and association membership
- A list of conferences at which you have given papers
- Any publications
- Other interests

Keep your CV up to date. If you have a computer, keep your CV on disc and add to it as things happen to you. Do not forget to keep backup copies. When you come to print (or type) it out, make sure that you use heavy paper and try to use paper of a standard size – preferably A4 (approximately 8.27 cm × 11.69 cm).

KNOW YOURSELF	**Questions about this section**				
1	I do not feel I have done enough to fill a CV	SA	A	U	D	SD
2	CVs are only necessary if you hold a senior position	SA	A	U	D	SD
3	Compiling a CV helps you to realise just how much you *have* achieved	SA	A	U	D	SD

■ SELF-PRESENTATION 2: APPEARANCE

How you appear to others is an important element of presentation of self. We can do little about our looks, we can do a little about our weight if we need to. One thing we can do a lot about is the way we dress. Often, people find a particular style of dressing, making up, wearing their hair and so on, early on in life. Everything after that is a modification of that style. Consider the way that you are dressed at the moment. Do you look reasonably up-to-date? Would you have comfortably fitted in to a group of people that existed 10 years ago? Review your own style and see the degree to which you need to make changes. You may feel that such things are not particularly important. They are when it comes to getting jobs, being asked to talk at conferences, being asked to teach groups of students. Whilst none of us has to conform completely, it is perhaps a bit arrogant to say that 'people will just have to accept me as I am'. In one sense they will – you will be you whatever happens. On the other hand, you can do much to work on your outward appearance.

EXERCISE	**Number 66**
Aim of exercise:	To explore the way that you look
Activity:	On a piece of paper, write out a description of the way you look. In other words, start your description along the following lines:
	'John Davies is tall . . .'
Variations:	If you are working in a group, discuss your individual reports and test the degree to which other people agree with your assessment of your appearance.

KNOW YOURSELF   Questions about this section

1	I take very little notice of fashion in clothes	SA	A	U	D	SD
2	I would like to be able to spend more money on the way that I look	SA	A	U	D	SD
3	It is less important that nurses look smart and more important that their care is excellent	SA	A	U	D	SD

■ **SELF-PRESENTATION 3: INTRODUCTIONS**

Imagine yourself meeting a group of three people that you have never met before. How would you introduce yourself? Would you automatically shake hands? Would you introduce yourself by name only or would you say something about yourself? Would you find the introduction easy to do? In the next exercise, we reflect on how you introduce yourself to others.

This is a fairly vital aspect of nursing given that most of us will have to meet numerous patients and new colleagues in the course of our working lives. Notice how other people introduce themselves and notice, too, the people that do it well.

EXERCISE	Number 67
Aim of exercise:	To explore how you introduce yourself to others
Activity:	Think of the following situations:

- A person is introduced to you at work
- You meet someone in a pub
- You are asked to introduce someone at a formal meeting

Read through those situations and then write down *exactly* what you would say in each of them. Notice the degree to which your manner of introduction varies or stays the same in each partnership. Notice, too, whether or not you:

- Introduce yourself by your first name, your second name or by both
- Shake hands and smile
- Say something about yourself
- Feel nervous

KNOW YOURSELF   Questions about this section

1	Introductions do not matter much; it's what comes after the introduction that matters	SA	A	U	D	SD
2	First impressions tend to be lasting ones	SA	A	U	D	SD
3	Many clinical staff are not particularly skilled in introducing themselves	SA	A	U	D	SD

■ SELF-PRESENTATION 4: USING THE TELEPHONE

Answering the telephone is another basic but vital skill. Consider the number of times that people communicate on the telephone and then reflect on the degree to which most people do it well. Think about the people that work on your ward or unit and notice how they *answer* the telephone. One day, try ringing your hospital from outside and try to imagine that you do not work there. What sort of impression of the hospital do you get?

EXERCISE	**Number 68**
Aim of exercise:	To explore your use of the telephone
Activity:	Imagine yourself in two situations:

- At home
- At work

Now write down *exactly* what you say when you answer the phone in these two places.

Reflect on what you have written down and answer the following questions:

When you are at home do you:
- Just say the phone number?
- Say 'hello'?
- Say your number and your name?

When you are at work do you:
- Just say the name of your ward or unit?
- Identify yourself by name?
- Use your first name?
- Identify yourself by grade?
- Sound enthusiastic?

Consider ways in which you could improve your telephone style. Think, too, about ways that you *finish* a phone conversation. Consider, carefully, how you take information over the phone and consider *always*:

- Summarising what is said by the other person *to* the other person
- Writing down what is said and repeating it back to the caller

Variations: It is interesting to video tape yourself and your colleagues answering the phone. Often we use a considerable amount of body language when we use the phone. Obviously, this is all missed by the person at the other end! My children are always highly amused by the fact that I wave one arm around in the air when I am slightly nervous in a telephone conversation. Try to notice your own idiosyncrasies.

1	People seem to change when they talk on the phone	SA	A	U	D	SD
2	I am fairly skilled in holding phone conversations and find this discussion rather unnecessary	SA	A	U	D	SD
3	Most people at the hospital I work in are not very effective in using the telephone	SA	A	U	D	SD

■ **SELF-PRESENTATION 5: COPING WITH OTHER PEOPLE'S EMOTIONS**

We care for people who are experiencing difficult life situations. The fact of being a patient at all can be difficult to live with. Being in hospital and working in hospital can take its toll on the emotions. Whilst some people prefer or choose to 'bottle up' their feelings, others will want to express them. Some general statements, drawn from the literature on the topic may be made:

- Emotional release is usually self-limiting. If the person is allowed to cry or get angry, that emotion will be expressed and then gradually subside. The supportive nurse will allow it to happen and not become unduly distressed by it.

- Physical support can sometimes be helpful in the form of holding the person's hand or putting an arm round them. Care should be taken, however, that such actions are unambiguous and that the holding of the patient or colleague is not too 'tight'. A very tight embrace is likely to inhibit the release of emotion. It is worth remembering, also, that not everyone likes or wants physical contact. It is important the nurse's support is not seen as intrusive by the patient or colleague.

- Once the person has had a release of emotion they will need time to piece together the insights that they gain from such release. Often all that is needed is that the nurse sits quietly with the client while he occasionally verbalises what he is thinking. The post cathartic period can be a very important stage in helping people with their emotions.

- There seems to be a link between the amount we can 'allow' another person to express emotion and the degree to which we can handle our own emotion. This is another reason why the nurse needs self-awareness. To help others explore their feelings we need, first, to explore our own. Many colleges and university departments offer workshops on cathartic work and self-awareness development that can help in both training the nurse to help others and in gaining self-insight.

Whilst the psychology literature is divided on whether or not emotional release is *always* a good thing, it seems likely that most of us feel better when we have had a chance to express our feelings. In western cultures, most people need to do this in some degree of privacy, in the company of someone they can trust and feel comfortable with. Bear in mind, though, that there are considerable cultural variations in the question of expressing emotions. People from the 'Latin' countries, for example express their feelings much more readily than do people from more Northern countries. Also, there is a lot of variation between different sorts of people and different sorts of personalities. Just as there are 'high touchers' and 'low touchers', so there are people who express emotion easily and those who do not. It seems unhelpful to suggest that everyone *should* express emotion.

EXERCISE	**Number 69**
Aim of exercise:	To explore how you handle emotional release in other people
Activity:	Try to recall a time in the recent past when someone began to cry in your company. What did you do? Did you:

- Put your arm round them?
- Reassure them and try to stop them crying?
- Allow them to cry?
- Get upset yourself?
- Start crying?
- Call someone else to help?
- Sit and say nothing?
- Something else, other than the above?

Read through the list of possibilities and consider the degree to which you feel you handled the situation well. How might you have handled it better? As a very general rule, most people seem to benefit from being allowed to express themselves and their emotions. Less harm seems to come from the expression of feelings than arises out of their being bottled up.

| Variations: | Again, if you are working in a group, discuss how each of you handled similar situations and try to draw up a simple procedure for helping other people with their emotions. This |

is not to suggest that we should become 'clinical' in our handling of other people but to note that if we know what to do *before* someone gets upset, we are more likely to help them when it happens.

The discussion of feelings in Chapter 4 of this book offers some ways of helping others express their emotions. The methods described for working on your *own* emotions, in that chapter, are also useful for helping other people.

KNOW YOURSELF	**Questions about this section**				
1	I cry fairly easily	SA	A	U	D	SD
2	I do not like it when other people get upset	SA	A	U	D	SD
3	People should release strong feelings in private	SA	A	U	D	SD

■ SELF-PRESENTATION 6: BEING ASSERTIVE

A considerable literature has developed on the idea of becoming more assertive. Being assertive means being able to state your wants and needs clearly and calmly without either finding yourself tongue tied and apologetic or aggressive and pushy. It is probably the case that we are more assertive in some situations with certain people than in others. Unfortunately, to date, nursing has not had a very good track record of encouraging people to be assertive, although the situation is changing.

John Heron [64] notes that when we have to confront another person about something, we tend to feel anxious. We are probably anxious because we do not know how the other person will react and are concerned that they might react in a negative way towards us. At base, none of us likes the idea of being rejected. Sometimes what stops us being assertive of confronting is this fear that the other person might think the less of us and as a result, reject us.

Heron suggests that because of this anxiety, we tend to react in one of two characteristic ways. Either we are aggressive and try to flatten the other person (the 'Sledgehammer' approach). Or we are mealy mouthed and never really get to assert ourselves at all (the 'pussyfooting' approach). The best approach probably lies someway between these two extremes. If we can learn to take a deep breath, forget our anxiety a little and learn to state what we want or need quietly, calmly and clearly, we are likely to get better results.

Assertiveness is often confused with being aggressive: there are important differences. The assertive person is the one who can state clearly and calmly what she wants to say, does not back down in the face of disagreement and is prepared to repeat what she has to say, if necessary. Woodcock and Francis [65] identify the following barriers to assertiveness:

1 *Lack of Practice*: you do not test your limits enough and discover whether you can be more assertive.
2 *Formative Training*: your early training by parents and others diminished your capacity to stand up for yourself.
3 *Being Unclear*: you do not have clear standards and you are unsure of what you want.
4 *Fear of Hostility*: you are afraid of anger or negative responses and you want to be considered reasonable.
5 *Undervaluing Yourself*: you do not feel that you have the right to stand firm and demand correct and fair treatment.
6 *Poor Presentation*: your self-expression tends to be vague, unimpressive, confusing or emotional.

Given that most nurses spend much of their time considering the needs of others, it seems likely that many overlook the personal needs identified within Woodcock and Francis' list of barriers to assertiveness. Part of the process of coping with stress is also the process of learning to identify and assert personal needs and wants. Snowball [66], developing the work of Dickson [67] and Smith [68] suggests a list of 'assertive rights' that can be a useful source of discussion. Whether or not you agree that they *are* rights is another interesting facet of the whole debate on assertiveness. Read through them and decide for yourself whether or not you feel you have them as a matter of right. Snowball's assertive rights are:

- I have the right to state my own needs and set my own priorities as a person, independently of others or of roles I assume
- I have the right to ask for what I want
- I have the right to be treated with respect as an intelligent, capable and equal human being
- I have the right to express my feelings, opinions and values
- I have the right to judge my own behaviour and take responsibility for the consequences of that behaviour
- I have the right to say 'No' or 'Yes' for myself
- I have the right to change my mind
- I have the right to say I do not understand and ask for more information
- I have the right to make mistakes and to take responsibility for those mistakes
- I have the right to interact with others without being dependent upon them for approval.

One thing is tricky about a list of rights. If we accept them as rights for ourselves, by implication, we also accept them as rights that other people have as well. This could sometimes lead to an interesting conflict. On the other hand, bear in mind that when you demonstrate assertive behaviour, you cannot rely on the other person exercising assertive behaviour too. They might act submissively and they might act aggressively. The chances are, though, that if you continue to act assertively, you are likely to find that your communication skills increase and people understand you better.

EXERCISE	**Number 70**
Aim of exercise:	To explore your level of assertiveness
Activity:	Consider the following situations and decide whether or not you feel you would be assertive in them. Consider, then, what it is about the *situation* and *about yourself* that stops you being assertive in some situations.

Situation	Assertive? (yes/no)
A friend rings you up and asks you to go out. You are not doing anything, but you don't want to go. You *want* to say 'no'.	
A senior nurse asks you to work overtime on one of your days off. You have already made other plans.	
The relationship you are in is going wrong. You want to end the relationship.	
You feel that another member of staff is taking advantage of you. You want to tell them to stop.	
A friend asks to borrow £5. She does not give it back. You need to ask her about it.	

EXERCISE	**Number 71**
Aim of exercise:	To explore the qualities of assertive people
Activity:	Try to think of four people that you know who you consider to be appropriately assertive. Then list the *specific behaviours* that mark them out as assertive. Consider, particularly, the following behaviours:

● Posture

- Proximity to other people
- Facial expression
- Use of gestures
- Tone of voice
- Eye contact
- Language used

Notice, too, the following issues:

- How they say 'no' to people
- How they manage to be assertive and remain popular
- How you know that they are *assertive* rather than *aggressive*
- The characteristics that *they* have that you could usefully copy

Variations:
If you are working in a group, discuss the behaviours and attitudes that go to make up effective assertive ways of living. Try, if you can, to role play situations that you have handled badly. Then, re-run the role play, playing an 'assertive' version. There are various publications that you can refer to for help with becoming assertive [69].

Richard Nelson-Jones [70] suggests that there are six possible areas of deficit in which you may have to build up your skills in order to act assertively.

1. *Being aware.* Sometimes it is a simple matter of realising that you *can* be assertive and that you have a *right* to make your own needs and wants clear.
2. *Overcoming mental barriers.* Often, we talk ourselves out of asserting ourselves because we feel that we shouldn't be assertive or that we may lose friendship as a result.
3. *Managing your anxiety.* Acting assertively tends to raise your anxiety level. The secret is to take a deep breath and carry on!
4. *Knowing what to say.* This is where rehearsal is useful. It helps if you can talk through, with a friend, the options that you are going to have in an anticipated situation in which you want to be assertive.
5. *Knowing how to say it.* You need to consider the *paralinguistic* aspects of speech: tone of voice, volume, pitch and so forth. You also need to think about how you *stand* or *sit* in relation to the person you are being assertive with.
6. *Acting appropriately.* It is important to back up what you say with what you *do*. It is one thing to be 'verbally assertive'. It is another to act out what you have said.

1	I tend to bottle things up and then blurt out whats *really* on my mind	SA	A	U	D	SD
2	Other people seem to have few problems with assertion	SA	A	U	D	SD
3	I think I am appropriately assertive	SA	A	U	D	SD

■ PERSONAL SKILLS

In coming to the conclusion of this book, it will be useful to clarify your *personal skills*: that is, those strengths, achievements and skills that you have acquired through the process of living. The final exercise asks you to identify your own skills through a range of categories. It is not an exhaustive personal audit but it can help you to identify areas of achievement and those areas that you still have to work on.

EXERCISE	**Number 72**
Aim of exercise:	To identify your personal skills
Activity:	Read through the list that follows and rate yourself against each item using the following code:

1 I am skilled in this
2 I am fairly skilled in this
3 I am not sure if I am skilled in this
4 I am not very skilled in this
5 I am not skilled at all in this

PERSONAL SKILLS	Your rating (1–5)
STUDY SKILLS – Essay writing – Taking notes – Keeping a database of references – Keeping up-to-date COMPUTING SKILLS – Formatting discs – Copying work to disc – Wordprocessing	

PERSONAL SKILLS	Your rating (1–5)

– Using a database
– Using a spreadsheet
– Working with graphics
 	
INTERPERSONAL SKILLS
– Listening
– Attending
– Using questions
– Reflection
– Empathy
– Checking for understanding
 	
ASSERTIVENESS
– Clearly stating my needs and wants
– Saying 'no' to other people
– Appropriately complimenting others
– Disagreeing with other people
– Returning goods to a shop
– Challenging others
 	
SOCIAL SKILLS
– Introducing myself to other people
– Introducing others
– Maintaining a conversation with
  relative strangers
 	
NURSING SKILLS
– Care planning
– Practical clinical skills
– Skills in working with adults
– Skills in working with the elderly
– Skills in working with children
– Skills in working with the mentally ill
– Skills in working with the mentally
  handicapped
 	
NURSING KNOWLEDGE
– Knowledge of nursing theory (including
  nursing models)
– Knowledge of the biological sciences
– Knowledge of the social sciences
– Knowledge of ethics
– Knowledge of medicine
– Knowledge of pharmacology
– Knowledge of teaching and learning
  methods	

PERSONAL SKILLS	Your rating (1–5)
RELATIONSHIPS – Skills in close relationships – Skills in working with people of the same sex – Skills in working with people of the opposite sex – Skills in beginning relationships – Skills in finishing relationships – Skills in relationships with patients – Skills in relationships with colleagues – Skills in relationships with friends	

■ SUMMARY OF THIS CHAPTER

This chapter has explored a range of issues surrounding how you present yourself to others. Specifically, it has explored:

- How to write your CV
- Appearance
- Introductions
- Using the telephone
- Coping with other people's emotions
- Being assertive
- Personal skills

10 | A Miscellany of Self-Awareness Activities

The road of excess leads to the palace of wisdom.

WILLIAM BLAKE

Keywords	● Awareness
	● Creativity
	● Mantras
	● Cultural differences
	● Values clarification

Aims of this chapter	● To explore other ways of getting to know yourself
	● To encourage creativity
	● To explore the use of mantras
	● To examine your acknowledgement of the culturally different
	● To explore personal values

In this final chapter, a range of activities for exploring aspects of yourself are described. In Hermann Hesse's novel, *Steppenwolf*, the hero comes across a door marked NOT FOR THE UNINITIATED and has to decide whether or not to go through it. This chapter is not quite as dramatic as that but it is recommended that you work through the other activities in the book before you move on to these. On the other hand, if you do not like being directed in this sort of way, why not *start* here! Also, try to suspend disbelief as you work through these activities: because some of them are different, there is sometimes a tendency to reject them out of hand. Try them — see what happens.

Most of the activities in this section require you to take a little time to reflect and even dream. You may find that these activities take a little longer than some of the others. Also, you may want to expore these exercises in the company of another person or in a small group. If you do, note the degree to which you are prepared to self-disclose. What are you *not* telling the people in your group? It is often this 'hidden agenda' that is the most fruitful source of self-awareness.

EXERCISE	**Number 73**
Aim of exercise:	To explore the creative and intuitive aspects of yourself
Activity:	Simply read through the following questions and answer each of them, taking your time over the process. This activity is adapted from one used in gestalt therapy and one that is often used as an 'icebreaker' in group work.

1 If you were a piece of music, what piece would you be? Describe yourself as that.
2 If you were a flower, what flower would you be? Describe yourself as that.
3 If you were a country, what country would you be? Describe yourself as that.
4 If you were a book, what book would you be? Describe yourself as that.
5 If you were a painting, what painting would you be? Describe yourself as that.
6 If you were a period in history, what period would you be? Describe yourself as that.
7 If you were a member of the opposite sex, what would you be like? Describe yourself as that.
8 If you were another person, who would you be? Describe yourself as that.
9 If you were an animal, what would you be? Describe yourself as that.
10 If you were a building, what building would you be? Describe yourself as that.

EXERCISE	**Number 74**
Aim of exercise:	To explore the far reaches of your imagination and your sense of identity
Activity:	Read through the following statements and reflect on each. This exercise takes time and is not particularly easy.

1 Imagine yourself before you were born...
2 Imagine yourself after you are dead...
3 Imagine yourself entirely alone...
4 Imagine yourself as another person...
5 Imagine yourself as all powerful...
6 Imagine yourself as having no power at all...

EXERCISE	**Number 75**
Aim of exercise:	To explore your present mood
Activity:	Reflect on what mood you are in at the moment. The following list of moods may or may not help here:

Happy	Cheerful
Depressed	Anxious
Unhappy	Contented
Jumpy	Stressed
Agitated	Calm
Secure	Creative
Worried	Angry
Disappointed	Unsettled.
Settled	Enthusiastic

Whatever mood you identify yourself as being in, *exaggerate* it. Allow yourself to become that mood, only more so! As you do this, notice what happens to your mood. It may, for instance:

- Lift
- Get better
- Get worse
- Stay the same
- Change

Next, ask yourself what this mood is 'about' and listen to yourself for the answer. This process of 'exaggerating' moods can be useful in both identifying the sources of our moods and also, ironically, in helping to modify or change our mood. Try using it next time you are very anxious. The usual advice to an anxious person is to take some deep breaths and calm down. This is precisely what you *cannot* do when you are anxious! What you are good at, at that moment, is being anxious. In allowing yourself to be this, and in actively encouraging yourself in it, it is often possible to laugh at yourself and find yourself calming down. This method, sometimes called *paradoxical intention* has been developed as a psychotherapeutic technique known as logotherapy [71]

EXERCISE	**Number 76**
Aim of exercise:	To explore the notion of an 'inner guide'
Activity:	Some people believe that we have the answers to many of our problems within us. Some would say that we can be

helped by an 'inner guide' – an aspect of our 'real self'. This activity explores that notion. Stay open minded with this one.

Close your eyes and allow yourself to relax. Now imagine yourself slowly climbing a steep hill, towards a cave at the top. Take your time over the climb and do not rush to the top. Then, allow yourself to enter the cave and meet a solitary being who is able to answer all of your questions. You, however, are allowed only *one* question. Ask it of the person who has all the answers and listen carefully to the person's answer.

As you come back down the steep hill, reflect both on the question that you asked and on the answer that you 'received'. Once you have opened your eyes, reflect on your beliefs about what was 'happening' when you undertook the exercise.

This activity is adapted from a well known one used in psychosynthesis [72].

EXERCISE	**Number 77**
Aim of exercise:	To explore inner dialogue
Activity:	Sit in a quiet place and explore what Pearce [73] has called 'roof brain chatter'. This has been discussed in other chapters of this book. Simply sit and listen to the 'noise' that goes on inside your head. Allow yourself to notice all your passing thoughts and feelings. Do not attempt to follow any one of them but merely notice them, almost as an impartial observer. Notice any tendency you have to have an internal dialogue or an 'argument' with yourself. Notice different thoughts, value systems and tendencies to judge. Notice, too, any resistance you have towards carrying on with the exercise. Most important of all, notice at what point you *stop* doing the activity. After you stop, reflect on what it was like to do this exercise.

EXERCISE	**Number 78**
Aim of exercise:	To write your own epitaph
Activity:	When famous people die, the television companies and the newspapers already have pre-prepared obituaries written for them. How would *you* like to be remembered? For this exercise, you are required to write your own obituary or

epitaph. Thus, you piece starts:

'Rhys Williams was...'
When you have written it, reflect on what it felt like to consider yourself in the past tense in this way. Also, what were the *particular* things that stand out in your life to date?

EXERCISE	**Number 79**
Aim of exercise:	To explore creative aspects of yourself.
Activity:	In this exercise, all you are required to do is to complete the following sentences as completely as you can:

- If I was rich I would...
- If I was famous I would...
- What stops me being more successful is...
- If I was a pop star I would...
- If I ran the local health authority I would...
- If I was an artist I would...
- If I was very different I would...

EXERCISE	**Number 80**
Aim of exercise:	To explore the use of mantras as an aid to self-awareness
Activity:	This activity is for the more adventurous! Here, you are required to experiment with the use of a mantra as an aid to meditation. A mantra is a particular word or phrase that is repeated over and over again as an aid to stilling and calming the mind. Many religious and mystical traditions use repetitious phrases as part of their rituals and sometimes the mantra is a sacred sound or expression. Examples of mantras drawn from various traditions are as follows:

- *om* (pronounced 'aum'). This is probably the best known of all mantras and the most widely used.
- *om namah shivaya*. This is a traditional Indian mantra and translates, roughly, as 'I honour my own self' or, more literally, 'I bow to Shiva'.
- *om mani padme hum*. This is usually translated as 'The Jewel in the Lotus'.
- *la ilaha illa llah*. This is a line from the Koran and means: 'There is no God but Allah.
- *kyrie eleison*. This is a Greek phrase, used widely in the Christian tradition.

Smith and Wilks [74] suggest that the following phrases

could be used as Christian mantras:

- Be still and know that I am God
- Lord Jesus Christ, son of God, have mercy on me
  Stoll [75] offers a series of phrases that can be used in contemplative and meditation work. She divides these up according to various religions, as follows:

For Roman Catholic and Other Christian Traditions:

- Variations on the prayer: 'Our Father who art in heaven' or 'Hallowed be Thy Name'.
- Phrases from the Hail Mary: 'Hail Mary, full of grace...'.
- A phrase from Mary's Magnificat, *Luke* 1: 46–55: 'My soul magnifies the Lord'.

For Protestants:

- Psalm 23: 'The Lord is my Shepherd'.
- Psalm 100: 'Make a joyful noise unto the Lord'.
- Jesus' teachings or words: 'My peace I give to you' (*John* 4: 27) or 'Love one another' (*John* 15: 12),
  Other meaningful passages from the New Testament, such as 'The peace which passes all understanding' (*Phil.* 4: 7) or 'We have the mind of Christ' (1 *Cor.* 2: 16).

For Jewish People:

- The Hebrew word for *peace*: Shalom.
- The Hebrew word for *one*: Echod.
- Passages from the Old Testament such as 'You shall love your neighbour' (*Lev.* 19: 18) or God said 'Let there be light' (*Gen.* 1: 3).
- Phrases that conform to King David's practice of meditating on God's promises, precepts, law, works, wonders, name and decrees,

For Moslems:

- The Word for God, 'Allah'; 'The Lord is wondrous kind'...
- Adahum 'One God' the words of the first Moslem who called the 'faithful' to prayer.

For Hindus and Buddhists:

- The Bhagavad Gita, the Hindu Scriptures, says, 'Joy is inward'.
- Part of a favourite invocation of Hindu priests, 'Thou art everywhere' and 'Thou art without form'.
- Buddhist literature contains phrases like these: 'Life is a journey' and 'I surrender indifferently'.

Still others prefer single words or even meaningless sounds. Words and expressions that have been used as mantras include:

- Peace

- Love
- Harmony
- Be here now
- I am one

Once you have selected a mantra that suits your personality and/or belief system, find somewhere quiet to meditate. Sit down and close your eyes. Take a few deep breaths and begin to slowly repeat the mantra over and over, for about twenty minutes. If your are distracted by other thoughts or feelings, simply bring yourself back to repeating the mantra.

Try to repeat this meditational activity every day for at least 3 weeks. Notice to what degree the use of a mantra brings you insight into any aspect of yourself, whether from the point of view of how stressed you are or from a more profound, spiritual point of view. Mantras are not for everyone but some people find them to be a potent means of reducing stress whilst others imbue them with considerable religious and mystical significance.

EXERCISE	**Number 81**
Aim of exercise:	To explore your sensitivity towards the culturally different
Activity:	As nurses we work with people from a variety of cultures. Read through the following list of suggestions about working with the culturally different, adapted from the work of Tappen [76], and identify the degree to which you do or do not observe these guidelines.

- Learn more about cultural beliefs, values and practices
- Resist seeing everyone from a particular culture as being alike
- Interpret behaviour on the basis of its meaning to the other person and that person's culture
- Be prepared to adjust your own behaviour in the presence of someone from another culture
- Distinguish between behaviour that needs to be changed and behaviour that can be accommodated

---

EXERCISE	**Number 82**
Aim of exercise:	To explore your values
Activity:	This exercise helps you to clarify what it is you believe strongly about: what the Americans call 'values clarification' [77]. Read through the following list and identify which of the statements you agree with. Then work through the items and

ponder on *why* you agree with some and disagree with others. Try to find the reasoning behind your values.

	Agree/disagree
People should be free to choose whether or not they have abortions	
Everyone should be allowed to follow the religious faith of their choice	
People should tell the truth at all costs	
War is always wrong	
Gay people should be allowed to marry	
Prison sentences are generally too lenient	
People should be allowed to make as much money as they can	
Euthanasia is always wrong	
All religions have some truth in them	

This completes the exploration of self as far as this book is concerned. As far as you and I are concerned, the task never ends. I hope that you have found the activities in this book useful and interesting: return to them again at a later date and see whether your responses to them are the same or different. All of us need to continue to develop our sense of self. We have no choice in this: we *are* changing! The point is to have some say in the process and to be aware of it. I let Colin Wilson have the final word:

> The basic problem of human existence is so simple that no philosopher has succeeded in stating it. People do not spend their time 'weighing up existence' in order to get through the average working day. And yet everything we do betrays a basic attitude to life, revealing that, in a certain sense, everything *has* been weighed up and judged. A man's handwriting, even the way he ties his shoelace, reveals his character, and character itself is nothing less than a series of acts that 'pass judgement' on human life. [78]

Appendix I:
Self-Awareness Questionnaire

The following questionnaire is made up of questions that have been used with a variety of groups of health professionals. The questions may be used in different ways. You may just want to read through them and answer them for yourself. Note the ones that you have difficulty with and notice the degree to which you are being honest with yourself. The questions can also be used with your working with another person. Using them this way, you each work through the questionnaire and answer alternate questions. Yet another way is to use the questions in a group context with each person being asked questions from the list by other group members.

How would you describe yourself to another person?
What sort of person do you think you appear to be to others?
What do you like to do most in your spare time?
Do you enjoy your work?
What do you like most about yourself?
What do you like least about yourself?
What kinds of music do you like listening to?
What kinds of books do you like reading?
Do you like poetry?
Do you drink alcohol regularly?
Do you go to concerts?
Do you often go to the cinema?
Do you manage money well?
What food do you like best?
Do you believe in God?
What particular skills do you have?
Do you play any sports?
Do you watch much television?
Would you say that you are an artistic person?
Would you say that you are an intelligent person?
Are you shy?
Do you get embarrassed easily?
What do you plan to do in the future?
What sort of relationship do you (or did you) have with your parents?
What do you worry about most?
How many friends do you have?

What are your favourite qualities in other people?
What are your political views?
What are your views on abortion?
Do you have a satisfactory sex life?
Who do you feel responsible for?
Do you feel that you earn enough money?
How do you feel about the way that you look?
How do you feel about the way that you dress?
What time do you go to bed at night?
What are the biggest disappointments of your life to date?
What are your greatest achievements?
Do you belong to any clubs or groups?
Do you have any hobbies?
Do you cook regularly?
Do you worry about your health?
Would you call yourself an optimist?
Do you often compare yourself with other people?
Do you feel that other people like you?
What do you most dislike in other people?
What sort of parent do you (or would you) make?
Would you say that you self-disclose easily?
What do you feel most guilty about?
What are you most sensitive about?
What sorts of behaviour irritate you the most?
Do you day-dream a lot?
Would you say that you were a logical person?
What stresses you most?
If you could change yourself, what would you change?

Appendix II:
A Sample Curriculum Vitae

Name:	Sian Davies
Address:	24 Cathays Road
	Canton
	Cardiff
	CF8 1NY
Date of Birth:	18.4.69
Nationality:	British
Marital Status:	Single
Current Post:	Staff Nurse

Secondary Education:

Cardiff Grammar School, Lewis Road, Cardiff   1980–1986

Further Education:

Cardiff Polytechnic, Cowbridge Road, Cardiff   1986–1987

Professional Training and Education:

Cardiff Royal Infirmary: Registered General Nurse Course: 1987–1990

Qualifications: 5 'O' Level GCEs:

English Language
Welsh
Mathematics
Chemistry
Art   Obtained in 1985

2 'A' Level GCEs:

Mathematics
Chemistry   Obtained in 1986

Certificate in Business Studies   Obtained in 1987

Registered General Nurse   Obtained in 1990

Other Professional Training:

Attendance at residential workshop: Basic Counselling Skills: Sophia Conference Centre, Cardiff   1990

Present Post:
Staff Nurse, Psychogeriatric Day Unit, Cardiff General Hospital

Outline of Responsibilities in Present Post:
I am responsible for planning and organising care for a group of six elderly women who have a variety of medical problems. We are currently introducing a primary nursing programme.

I have introduced a teaching programme on the unit and help in the drawing up of learning contracts with students who work in the unit. I also carry out primary interviews when students start work on the unit.

Other Work Experience:
Holiday work as a Care Assistant, Canton Residential Home, Canton, Cardiff: Summer 1984 and Summer 1985

Publication:
Davies, S. 1989 Who cares for the elderly? *Nursing Gazette*: 3: 4: 12–14.

Conference Paper:
2nd National Nursing Conference, University of Wales College of Medicine, Cardiff: *Primary Nursing and the Elderly*: July 1990.

Special Skills:
Typing skills: 60 wpm
Wordprocessing Skills (WordPerfect and Wordstar)
General computing skills: spreadsheets, graphics, database development (Dbase)
Driving Licence

Professional Activities:
Member of the Royal College of Nursing
Member of the South Glamorgan Nursing Research Interest Group
Member of the British Association for Counselling

Interests:
Canoeing
Swimming
Reading

Awards:
Best Student in Computing Award: Cardiff Polytechnic: 1987

The RCN Student Award for Nursing Essays: *Planning Primary Nursing With the Elderly*: 1990

Appendix III:
Focus of Targets for 'Health For All' by the Year 2000 in Europe [79]

Targets 1–12: Health for All

1   Equity in health
2   Adding years to life
3   Better opportunities for the disabled
4   Reducing disease and disability
5   Eliminating measles, polio, neonatal tetanus, congenital rubella, diphtheria, congenital syphilis and indigenous malaria
6   Increasing life expectation at birth
7   Reduced infant mortality
8   Reducing maternal mortality
9   Combating disease of the circulation
10 Combating cancer
11 Reducing accidents
12 Stopping the increase in suicide

Targets 13–17: Life Styles Conducive to Health For All

13 Developing healthy public policies
14 Developing social support systems
15 Improved knowledge and motivation for health behaviour
16 Promoting positive health behaviour
17 Decreasing health-damage behaviour

Targets 18–25: Producing Healthy Environments

18 Policies for health environments
19 Monitoring, assessment and control of environmental risks
20 Controlling water pollution
21 Protecting against air pollution
22 Improving food safety
23 Protecting against hazardous wastes
24 Improving housing conditions
25 Protecting against work-related health risks

Targets 26–31: Providing Appropriate Care

26   A health care system based on primary health care
27   Distribution of resources according to need
28   Re-orientating primary medical care
29   Developing teamwork
30   Co-ordinating services
31   Ensuring quality of services

Targets 32–38: Support for Health Development

32   Developing a research base for health for all
33   Implementing policies for health for all
34   Management and delivery of resources
35   Health information systems
36   Training and deployment of staff
37   Education of people in non-health sectors
38   Assessment of health technologies

Appendix IV:
Self-Awareness Checklists

SELF-AWARENESS CHECKLIST NUMBER 1

Problem Solving

A structured approach to dealing with problems can often help to reduce stress. Adapting the work of Cranwell-Jones (1987), the following stages of problem solving can be identified and worked through:

1 *Identify the problem clearly.* The more specific you can be about what really is the problem, the better.
2 *Collect data of relevance to the problem.* You need to list all the relevant facts about all aspects of the problem.
3 *Analyse the data you collect.* Calm sifting through of all of the issues involved will help you to appreciate all sides of the problem. It may help to talk things through with someone else at this stage, too.
4 *Generate possible solutions to the problem.* Allow yourself to think of *all* possible solutions. Take your time over this stage. The many solutions, both practical and impractical that you can generate, the better.
5 *Evaluate the alternatives and select a solution to the problem.* From all of the possible, solutions, identify the one that you want to use.
6 *Develop an action plan.* Having identified your solution, plan a course of action to achieve it.
7 *Implement the action plan.*
8 *Review the outcome.*

Cranwell-Jones, J. 1987 *Managing Stress*: Gower, Aldershot.

SELF-AWARENESS CHECKLIST NUMBER 2

Assert Yourself

It is easy in nursing to be subservient to the needs of others. Woodcock and Francis (1982) suggest that research indicates that assertive people tend to:

- Avoid confused emotions
- Be simple in their dealings with others
- Carry through what they set out to do
- Not put themselves down
- Watch out for 'flak'
- Acknowledge that error does not weaken
- Go out to win

Woodcock, M. and Francis, D. 1982 *The Unblocked Manager: A Practical Guide to Self-Development*: Gower, Aldershot.

SELF-AWARENESS CHECKLIST NUMBER 3

Be More Open

Some people, when they are stressed, tend to become more introverted. Consider opening up and sharing yourself more with others. Some areas in which you might consider becoming more open include:

- In personal relationships
- In relationships with colleagues
- In relationships with clients
- In talking to seniors
- In seeking assessment from your boss
- In admitting mistakes

SELF-AWARENESS CHECKLIST NUMBER 4

Behavioural Relaxation Training

Schilling and Poppen (1983) describe a procedure they call Behavioural Relaxation Training. This includes the use of following 10 instructions for assessing relaxation:

1 Breathing: relaxed
2 Voice: quiet
3 Body: no movement of the trunk
4 Head: in midline, supported by recliner
5 Eyes: closed with smooth eyelids
6 Jaw: dropped, with lips parted

7   Throat: no movement or swallowing
8   Shoulders: sloped and even, no movement
9   Hands, curled in resting posture
10 Feet: pointed away from each other, forming a 90 degree angle

These 10 criteria can be used as a personal check list to assess the effectiveness of some of the relaxation exercises described in this book, when those exercises are carried out whilst lying down.

Schilling, D. and Poppen, R. 1983 Behavioural relaxation training and assessment. *Journal of Behaviour Therapy and Experimental Psychiatry*: 14: 99–107.

SELF-AWARENESS CHECKLIST NUMBER 5

Preventing Stress at Work

All aspects of work in nursing can be potentially stressful. Atkinson (1988) suggests the following points for tackling job related stress:

1   Ensure a good person-job fit or make necessary adjustments
2   Develop sensible, rational beliefs and attitudes to yourself, your performance and your job
3   Change your behaviour in line with your new attitudes, including reviewing priorities
4   Develop the right skills and behaviours to enable you to do your job to the best of your ability
5   Develop a good social support network, both at work and with family and friends
6   Keep as physically healthy as you can through sensible diet, sleep, exercise and so forth
7   Learn to relax
8   Learn to use leisure time sensibly

Atkinson, J.M. 1988 *Coping with Stress at Work: How to Stop Worrying and Start Succeeding*: Thorsons, Wellingborough.

SELF-AWARENESS CHECKLIST NUMBER 6

Taking a Balanced Approach to Stress Management

Meg Bond (1986) suggests four basic approaches to the management of stress:

1   Mental and physical distraction. Here, the person adopts various strategies to cope with stress through distraction.

2 Self-nurturance. Here, the person is more concerned with looking after herself as an approach to coping.
3 Confronting the problem. The approach, here is a rational, problem-solving one.
4 Emotional expression. Stress is dealt with by exploring the effect it has on feelings.

A balanced approach to stress management may be one that draws on all four approaches. Consider your own strategies for coping with stress. Do you favour one approach rather than the others? If so, could you benefit from considering other methods?

Bond, M. 1986 *Stress and Self-Awareness: A Guide for Nurses*: Heinemann, London.

SELF-AWARENESS CHECKLIST NUMBER 7

Help With Writing

Nearly all nurses have to write: reports, letters, papers, articles and so on. Many people find the process of writing difficult and stressful. If we can learn to express ourselves clearly and easily in writing, we may save ourselves the stress of rewriting and editing. Robert Gunning (1968) offers 10 principles of clear writing:

- Keep sentences short
- Prefer the simple to the complex
- Prefer the familar word
- Avoid unnecessary words
- Put action in your verbs
- Write like you talk
- Use terms your reader can picture
- Tie in with your reader's experience
- Make full use of variety
- Write to express not impress

These principles can be used for any sort of writing from student projects to research reports and from papers for publication to day-to-day correspondence.

Gunning, R. 1968 *The Technique of Clear Writing*: 2nd edition: McGraw Hill, London.

SELF-AWARENESS CHECKLIST NUMBER 8

Develop Flexibility

Stress can make us inflexible and resistant to change. Woodcock and Francis (1981) suggest that several skills are combined in the capacity to be flexible:

- Accurately assessing situations
- Listening to others
- Continuously redefining the present
- Not longing for 'the good old days'
- Enjoying challenge
- Admitting errors to oneself

Woodcock, M. and Francis, D. 1981 *The Unblocked Manager: A Practical Guide to Self-Development*: Gower, Aldershot.

SELF-AWARENESS CHECKLIST NUMBER 9

The Concept of Personhood

What does it mean to be a person? This is a theme that has been developed throughout this book. You may want to consider Bannister and Fransella's (1986) criteria for being a person. They are:

1 You entertain a notion of your own separateness from others: you rely on the privacy of your own consciousness.
2 You entertain a notion of the integrality or completeness of your experience, so that all parts of it are relatable because you are the experiencer.
3 You entertain a notion of your own continuity over time; you possess your own biography and live in relation to it.
4 You entertain a notion of the causality of your actions; you have purposes, you intend, you accept a partial responsibility for the effects of what you do.
5 You entertain a notion of other persons by analogy with yourself; you assume a comparability of subjective experience.

Bannister, D. and Fransella, F. 1986 *Inquiring Man*: 3rd Edition: Croom Helm, London.

SELF-AWARENESS CHECKLIST NUMBER 10

Speedreading

One of the things that can help you to study more effectively and thus know what you want and need to read is faster reading. Palmer and Pope (1984) offer the following six-point programme for faster reading:

1 Read the headings, sub-headings and (where appropriate) chapter titles,

2   Read the introduction, the conclusion and any interim summaries there may be,
3   Read/peruse any graphs, illustrations, diagrams and tables
4   Read the *first* and *last* sentences of each paragraph
5   Fill in remaining gaps (read it through in the 'normal', A–Z fashion)
6   Review and clear problems

Palmer, R. and Pope, C. 1984 *Brain Train: Studying for Success*: Spon, London.

SELF-AWARENESS CHECKLIST NUMBER 11

What is a Relationship?

Hinde (1979) describes what constitutes a relationship in the following way. It is interesting to read through the checklist and decide to what degree and with whom you have relationships.

- There is intermittent interaction between two people
- The interaction involves interchanges over an extended period of time
- These interchanges have some degree of mutuality
- This mutuality does not necessarily imply cooperation
- There is also some degree of continuity between successive interactions

Hinde R.A. 1979 *Towards Understanding Relationships*: Academic Press, London.

SELF-AWARENESS CHECKLIST NUMBER 12

The Benefits and Bonuses of Exercise

Part of the process of coming to know yourself is caring for yourself. The Health Education Council (1979) suggests that the benefits and bonuses of taking exercise are as follows:

- Exercise improves the staying power of your heart and circulation and may protect you against coronary heart disease
- It keeps your neck, back and joints supple and your posture right
- It tightens flabby muscles and gives you strength
- It helps you stay slim
- It helps to combat stress

- It can be great fun
- And it helps you feel good, in mind as well as body.

Health Education Council 1979 *Looking After Yourself*: Health Education, London.

SELF-AWARENESS CHECKLIST NUMBER 13

Counselling Skills Tool Kit

Counselling Skills are part of every nurse's repertoire. In becoming more self-aware we are often more able to help others come to terms with or solve their own personal problems. The following are the basic skills involved in the person-centred approach to counselling:

- Listening and attending
- Open questions
- Closed questions
- Reflection of feelings
- Reflection of content
- Checking for understanding
- Empathy development

SELF-AWARENESS CHECKLIST NUMBER 14

A Bill of Rights For Young People

The people of New York State have drawn up a bill of rights for children and young people. Consider the degree to which you feel that it is both exhaustive and necessary. Reflect, too, on the degree to which *you* were able to exercise such rights.

We, the people of New York State, believe in the right of every child to:

1 Affection, love, guidance and understanding from parents and teachers
2 Adequate nutrition and medical care to aid mental, physical and social growth
3 Free education to develop individual abilities and to become a useful member of society
4 Special care of the handicapped
5 Opportunity for recreation in a wholesome well-rounded environment
6 An environment that reflects peace and mutual concern
7 The opportunity for sound moral development

8   Constructive discipline to help develop responsibility
    and character
9   Good adult examples to follow
10 A future commensurate with abilities and aspirations
11 Enjoyment of all these rights, regardless of race,
    creed, sex, religion, national or social origin

Young People's Bill of Rights, New York State
Division for Youth, 84 Holland Avenue, NY 12208,
USA.

SELF-AWARENESS CHECKLIST NUMBER 15

Blocks to Learning

Sometimes we are our own worst enemies. We put
obstacles in the way of our learning by holding
certain irrational beliefs. Consider the degree to
which you live out the following four beliefs that Guy
Claxton argues get in the way of 'adults' learning:

- I must be *competent*
- I must be *in control*
- I must be *consistent*
- I must be *comfortable*

Claxton, G. 1986 *Live and Learn*: Harper and Row,
London.

Notes and References

1 Quoted in: Gersie, A. and King, N. 1990 *Storymaking in Education and Therapy*: Jessica Kingsley Publishers, London and Stockholm Institute of Education Press, Stockholm.

This is a magnificent book, full of details about myths, legends and stories. The authors bring back the skills of storytelling and offer a variety of ways of helping you to think about your own myths and stories.

2 Egan, G. 1990 *The Skilled Helper*: 4th Edition: Brooks/Cole, Monterey.

This is a useful and thorough book on a three stage model of counselling. Other books on counselling skills that you may find helpful are:

Burnard, P. 1989 *Counselling Skills for Health Professionals*: Chapman and Hall, London.

Murgatroyd, S. 1986 *Counselling and Helping*: Methuen, London.

Tschudin, V. 1986 *Counselling Skills for Nurses*: 2nd Edition: Balliere Tindall, London.

Dryden, W., Charles-Edwards, D. and Woolfe, R. (eds) 1989 *Handbook of Counselling in Britain*: Routledge, London.

3 Heron, J. 1973 *Experimental Training Techniques*: Human Potential Research Project, University of Surrey, Guildford.

This booklet, available direct from the University of Surrey contains many exercises for self-awareness development in groups.

Heron has continued his theme of the use of self in other, similar, publications. See, for example:

Heron, J. 1977a *Catharsis in Human Development*: Human Potential Resource Group, University of Surrey, Guildford.

Heron, J. 1977b *Behaviour Analysis in Education and Training*: Human Potential Research Group, University of Surrey, Guildford.

4 Peplau, H. 1957 Therapeutic Concepts. In S.A. Smoyak and S. Rouslin: *A Collection of Classics in Psychiatric Nursing Literature*: Slack, Thorofare, New Jersey.

5 Kelly, G.A. 1955 *The Psychology of Personal Constructs*: Vols 1 and 2: Norton, New York.

6 Rogers, C.R. 1967 *On Becoming a Person*: Constable, London.

Carl Roger's book is made up of a series of essays about the process known as Client Centred Counselling. His writing style is easy and the book is a valuable resource for anyone studying interpersonal skills. An earlier work outlines the principles of the client-centred approach:

Rogers, C.R. 1951 *Client-Centred Therapy*: Constable, London.

7   Jourard, S. 1964 *The Transparent Self*: Van Nostrand, New York.
   Although this book is more than 20 years old, it is still an important account of how self-disclosure can help in helping others. Jourard has some important things to say about self-disclosure in nursing.

8   Schlenker, B.R. 1980 *Impression Management: The Self-Concept, Social Identity and Interpersonal Relations*: Brooks/Cole, Monterey.
   This important book, currently out of print, is a useful account of various theories of how we present ourselves to others. Order it through your library.

9   Tanner, D. 1986 *That's Not What I Meant!: How Conversational Style Makes or Breaks Your Relations With Others*: Dent, London.
   A particularly easy to read book about linguistics – not normally a subject for light reading!

10   Rogers, C.R. 1967 *On Becoming a Person*: Constable, London. Rogers, C.R. 1983 *Freedom to Learn for the Eighties*: Merrill, Columbus, Ohio.

11   Sartre, J.-P. 1964 *Nausea*: Penguin, Harmondsworth.

12   Hesse, H. 1979 *My Belief*: Panther, St Albans.

13   Sartre, J.-P. 1969 *Words*: Penguin, Harmondsworth.

14   Wilson, C. 1965, 1978 *The Outsider*: Picador, London.
   Wilson was to follow this up with another book about the outsider in literature: Wilson, C. 1965 *Beyond the Outsider: a Philosophy of the Future*: Pan, London.

15   Weil, S. 1950 *Waiting on God*: Collins, Glasgow.

16   Gunner, A. 1990 Are We Handicapped By Our Sexual Prejudices? In Horne, E. (ed.) *Effective Communication*: Austen Cornish, London.

17   Jung, C.G. 1978 *Selected Writings*: Edited by A. Storr: Fontana, London.
   This is a particularly useful introduction to Jung's work. Jung was a prolific writer and his collected works span 20 volumes. Not all of his writing is clear to the lay reader. This selection offers extracts from the whole span of his work.

18   Polanyi, M. 1958 *Personal Knowledge*: University of Chicago Press, Chicago.

19   Hall, C. 1954 *A Primer of Freudian Psychology*: Mentor Books, New York.

20   Segal, J. 1985 *Phantasy in Everyday Life: a Psychoanalytical Approach to Understanding Ourselves*: Penguin, Harmondsworth.

21   Luft, J. 1969 *Of Human Interaction: The Johari Model*: Mayfield, Palo Alto.

22   Berne, E. 1964 *Games People Play*: Penguin, Harmondsworth.

Berne, E. 1972 *What Do You Say After You Say Hello?*: Corgi, London.

See, also: Harris, T. 1973 *I'm OK, You're OK*: Pan, London.

23   Pearce, J.C. 1981 *The Bond of Power: Meditation and Wholeness*: Routledge and Kegan Paul, London.

This is an intriguing book about Pearce's experiences with meditation and the development of his self-enlightenment.

24   Daniels, V. and Horowitz, L.J. 1984 *Being and Caring: A Psychology for Living*: 2nd Edition: Mayfield, Mountain View, California.

Daniels and Horowitz's book offers a considerable range of ideas about the caring within the framework of humanistic psychology. It is also packed with practical activities and exercises.

25   Turk, C. 1985 *Effective Speaking: Communicating in Speech*: Spon, London.

This is an interesting book for all sorts of reasons. First, it is clearly written. Second, it brings together a variety of psychological principles about communication in a readable format. Finally, it is an excellent guide to how to improve the way you project yourself.

26   Buzan, T. 1974 *Use Your Head*: BBC, London.

Still an essential and different book about how to study.

27   Some wordprocessors such as WordPerfect and WordStar have built-in outliners. Others are available as separate programs. One, PC-Outline is offered as Shareware. That means you can try it out for the cost of the disc and send a small amount of money to the author if you decide to continue to use it.

28   DBase, DataPerfect, PC File, Masterfile, Paradox, Cardbox, FoxBase, Superbase, LocoFile, Aspect, Retrieve, Reflex, are all examples of database programs. Keep it simple: do not go for one of the bigger programs. They tend to be overly complicated and they cost a lot more money! Various database programs are available as Shareware. With this system, you can try out a program for the cost of the disc and if you like it and want to keep it, you send a small donation to the writer of the program. Many shareware programs are excellent and easily the equal of some commercial software.

29   Turk, C. and Kirkman, J. 1989 *Effective Writing: Improving Scientific, Technical and Business Communication*: 2nd Edition: Spon, London.

I think that this is one of the most useful books on writing that you can buy. It offers very clear and very detailed advice on all aspects of writing. I go back to it time and time again.

Palmer, R. and Pope, C. 1984 *Brain Train: Studying for Success*: Spon, London.

This book is slightly different. It is written by a lecturer and by a student. The combination produces a very practical and useful book on all aspects of study skills.

Becker, H .S. 1986 *Writing for Social Scientists: How to Start and Finish Your Thesis, Book or Article*: The University of Chicago Press, Chicago.

This is useful reading for anyone who has to write essays, projects or papers in a college or university.

30   Mills, C. Wright 1959 *The Sociological Imagination*: Oxford University Press, Oxford.

31   Rogers, C.R. 1967 *On Becoming a Person*: Constable, London.

32   Brookfield, S.D. 1987 *Developing Critical Thinkers: Challenging Adults to Explore Alternative Ways of Thinking and Acting*: Open University Press, Milton Keynes.

Increasingly, nurse education is adopting modern methods of adult learning. This book offers a valuable critique of many approaches to the education of adults and contains many practical suggestions for how to reorganise adult learning encounters.

33 Heron, J. 1977 *Catharsis in Human Development*: Human Potential Resource Project, University of Surrey, Guildford.

This book is not usually available from general bookshops. Send directly to the Human Potential Resource Project for it.

34 Reich, W. 1949 *Character Analysis*: Simon and Schuster, New York.

This is a hefty book and not the easiest to read. There are a number of books about Reich's work. A good one is:

Totton, N. and Edmonston, E. 1988 *Reichian Growth Work: Melting the Blocks to Life and Love*: Prism Press, Bridport.

35 Lowen, A. 1967 *Betrayal of the Body*: Macmillan, New York.

Lowen, A. and Lowen, L. 1977 *The Way to Vibrant Health: a Manual of Bioenergetic Exercises*: Harper and Row.

36 Keleman, H. 1984 Attitudes are alive and well and gainfully employed in the sphere of action. *American Psychologist* 29: 310–335.

Keleman has developed the Lowen's ideas about bioenergetics and it is interesting to compare the two approaches to working through the body towards the expression of feelings.

37 Perls, F., Hefferline, R. and Goodman, P. 1951 *Gestalt Therapy*: Penguin, Harmondsworth.

38 Heron, J. 1974 *Reciprocal Counselling Manual*: Human Potential Research Project, University of Surrey, Guildford.

Heron, J. 1982 *Educating the Affect*: Human Potential Research Project, University of Surrey, Guildford.

Jackins, H. 1970 *Fundamentals of Co-Counselling Manual*: Rational Island Publishers, Seattle, Washington.

39 Mishra, R. 1959 *Fundamentals of Yoga*: Julian Press, New York.

Hewitt, J. 1978 *Meditation*: Hodder and Stoughton, Sevenoaks.

40 Perls, F., Hefferline, R.F. and Goodman, P. 1951 *Gestalt Therapy: Excitement and Growth in the Human Personality*: Penguin, Harmondsworth.

Perls, F. 1969 *Gestalt Therapy Verbatim*: Real People Press, Lafayette, California.

Smith, E.W.L. (ed.) 1975 *The Growing Edge of Gestalt Therapy*: Citadel Press, Secaucus, New Jersey.

41 Rogers, C.R. 1967 *On Becoming a Person*: Constable, London

42 Benner, P. 1981 *The Expert Practitioner*: Addison Wesley, San Fransisco, California.

43 Jung, C.G. 1967 *Collected Works; Volume 8*: Routledge and Kegan Paul, London

44 Orage, A.R. 1974 *Consciousness: Animal, Human and Superhuman*: Thorsons, Wellingborough.

45 This opens up an interesting debate about *how much* it is possible to observe and see. Some people have suggested that it is possible to become aware of all sorts of subtle and rarely distinguished aspects of the world. They would argue that there is much more going on in the universe than we normally notice but that some of these 'goings on' are observable under certain circumstances. For a discussion of some of these issues, see:

Heron, J. 1977 *Practical Methods in Transpersonal Psychology*: Human Potential Research Project, University of Surrey, Guildford.

Heron, J. 1981 *Paradigm Papers*: Human Potential Research Project: University of Surrey, Guildford.

Vaughan, F. 1985 Discovering transpersonal identity. *Journal of Humanistic Psychology*: 25: 3: 13–38.

How far you will want to pursue this 'other world' approach to self-awareness will depend on your view of the universe, your ideas about philosophy and, perhaps, your religious beliefs.

46 Tart, C. 1975 *Altered States of Consciousness*: Wiley, New York.

Hewitt, J. 1978 *Meditation*: Hodder and Stoughton, Sevenoaks, Kent.
Bond, M. 1986 *Stress and Self-Awareness: a Guide for Nurses*: Heinemann, London.

47 Pearce, J.C. 1981 *The Bond of Power: Meditation and Wholeness*: Routledge and Kegan Paul, London.

48 Gendlin, E. 1981 *Focusing*: Bantam, New York.

Hales-Tooke, J. 1989 Focusing in therapy: focusing in life: self and society. *European Journal of Humanistic Psychology*: XVII: 6: 113–116.

49 Gersie, A. and King, N. 1990 *Storymaking in Education and Therapy*: Jessica Kingsley Publishers, London and Stockholm Institute of Education Press, Stockholm.
   This is a fascinating book about myths and tales from all over the world and suggests all sorts of activities that can be carried out to explore myth and legend in a personal and group context.

50 Jung, C.G. 1978 *Selected Writings*: Edited by A. Storr: Fontana, London.

51 Reed, A.W. 1982 *Aboriginal Myths, Legends and Fables*: Reed, Wellington, New Zealand.

52 Woodcock, M. and Francis, D. 1982 *The Unblocked Manager: A Practical Guide to Self-Development*: Gower, Aldershot.

53 Macleod-Clark, J., Kendall, S. and Haverty, S. 1990 Effective use of health education skills. In Horne, E. (ed.) *Effective Communication*: Austen Cornish, London.

54 Health Education Council 1979 *Looking After Yourself!* Health Education Council, London.

55 Bailey, R. and Clarke, M. 1989 *Stress and Coping in Nursing*: Chapman and Hall, London.
   This is a very detailed and useful book about research, theory and practical methods of overcoming stress in nursing.

56 Selye, H. 1956 *The Stress of Life*: 2nd Edition: McGraw Hill, New York.

Selye, H. 1975 *Stress Without Distress*: Cygnet Books, New York

Selye, H. 1976 *Stress in Health and Disease*: Butterworth, London.

57   Bond, M. 1986 *Stress and Self-Awareness: A Guide for Nurses*: Heinemann, London.

58   Ashton, J. and Seymour, H. 1988 *The New Public Health: The Liverpool Experience*: Open University, Milton Keynes.

59   World Health Organisation 1981 *Global Strategy for Health For All by the Year 2000*: WHO, Geneva.

See, also, other related WHO publications:

World Health Organisation 1978 *Alma Ata 1977 Primary Health Care*: WHO, Geneva.

WHO, Europe 1981 *Regional Strategy for Attaining Health For All by the Year 2000*. EUR/RC 3018 rev. 1. WHO, Copenhagen.

WHO, Europe 1984 *Health Promotion: A discussion document on the concepts and principles*: WHO, Copenhagen.

WHO, Europe 1985 *Targets for Health for All*: WHO, Copenhagen.

60   Heron, J. 1989 *The Facilitators' Handbook*: Kogan Page, London.

61   Burnard, P. 1989 *Counselling Skills for Health Professionals*: Chapman and Hall, London.

Schulman, E.D. 1982 *Intervention in Human Services: A Guide to Skills and Knowledge*: 3rd Edition: Mosby, Philadelphia.
   This is a particularly useful and detailed guide to nearly all aspects of interpersonal skills in the caring professions.

62   Kennedy, G. 1982 *Everything is Negotiable: How to Negotiate and Win*: Arrow, London.

63   For more details on negotiating, see: Scott, W. 1988 *Negotiating: Constructive and Competitive Negotiation*: Paradigm Publishing, London.

64   Heron, J. 1989 *Six Category Intervention Analysis*: Human Potential Resource Project, University of Surrey, Guildford

65   Woodcock, M. and Francis, D. 1982 *The Unblocked Manager: A Practical Guide to Self-Development*: Gower, Aldershot.
   A curious title but an excellent and practical guide to development of personal and management skills.

66   Snowball, J. 1989 Using assertiveness skills. In Vaughan, B. and Pillmoor, M. (eds) *Managing Nursing Work*: Scutari Press, London.

67   Dickson, A. 1982 *A Woman in Your Own Right: Assertiveness and You*: Quartet Books, London.

68   Smith, M. 1975 *When I Say No I Feel Guilty*: Bantam Books, New York.

69   Alberti and Emmons 1982 *Your Perfect Right: A Guide to Assertive Living*: Impact Publishers, San Luis, California.

Allan, J. 1989 *How to Develop Your Personal Management Skills*: Kogan Page, London.

Adler, R.B. 1977 *Confidence in Communication: A Guide to Assertive Social Skills*: Holt, Rinehart and Winston, London.

Clark, C. 1978 *Assertive Skills for Nurses*: Contemporary Publishing, Wakefield, Mass.

Corey, F. 1983 *I Never Knew I Had A Choice*: 2nd Edition: Brooks-Cole, California.

Dickson, A. 1985 *A Woman in Your Own Right: Assertiveness and You*: Quartet Books, London.

Ernst, S. and Goodison, L. 1981 *In Our Own Hands: A Book of Self-Help Therapy*: The Women's Press, London.

70 Nelson-Jones, R. 1986 *Human Relationship Skills: Training and Self-Help*: Cassell, London.

71 Victor Frankl developed this technique out of his experiences with people with particularly resistive problems. He realised that fighting feelings rarely works: to *encourage* them, seems to take the sting out of them. Frankl has written many books and papers on the use of this approach. A few of them are:

Frankl, V. 1959 *Man's Search for Meaning*: Beacon Press, New York.

Frankl, V. 1960 Paradoxical intention: A logotherapeutic technique. *American Journal of Psychotherapy*: 14: 520–35.

Frankl, V. 1969 *The Will to Meaning*: World Publishing: New York.

Frankl, V. 1978 *The Unheard Cry for Meaning*: Simon and Schuster, New York.

72 Ferruci, P. 1982 *What We May Be*: Turnstone Press, Wellingborough.

73 Pearce, J.C. 1981 *The Bond of Power: Meditation and Wholeness*: Routledge and Kegan Paul, London.

74 Smith, E. and Wilks, N. 1988 *Meditation*: Optima, London.

75 Stoll, R.I. 1989 Spirituality and chronic illness. In Carson, V.B. (ed.) *Spiritual Dimensions of Nursing Practice*: Saunders, Philadelphia.

76 Tappen, R.M. 1983 *Nursing Leadership: Concepts and Practice*: F.A. Davis, Philadelphia.
   This is a useful book about all aspects of nursing leadership and management. It deals with a range of topics from leadership styles and organisational management.

77 Simon, S.B., Howe, L.W. and Kirschenbaum, H. 1978 *Values Clarification: A Handbook of Practical Strategies for Teachers and Students*: Revised Edition: A and W Visual Library, New York.

78 Wilson, C. 1965 *Beyond the Outsider*: Pan, London.

79 WHO Europe 1985 *Targets for Health for All*: WHO, Copenhagen.

Bibliography

Adams-Webber, J. and Mancusco, J.C. (eds) *Applications of Personal Construct Theory*: Academic Press, London.

Adler, R.B. 1977 *Confidence in Communication: A Guide to Assertive Social Skills*: Holt, Rinehart and Winston, London.

Adler, R. and Rodman, G. 1988 *Understanding Human Communication*: 3rd Edition: Holt, Rinehart and Winston, New York.

Adler, R.B. and Towne, N. 1984 Looking out/looking in: *Interpersonal Communication*: Holt, Rinehart and Winston, London.

Adler, R.B., Rosenfield, L.B. and Towne, N. 1983 *Interplay: The Process of Interpersonal Communication*: Holt, Rinehart and Winston, London.

Alberti, R.E. and Emmons, M.L. 1982 *Your Perfect Right: A Guide to Assertive Living*: 4th Edition: Impact Publishers, San Luis.

Allan, D.M.E., Grosswald, S.J. and Means, R.P. 1984 Facilitating self-directed learning. In Green J.S., Grosswald, S.J., Suter, E. and Walthall, D.B. (eds) *Continuing Education for the Health Professions*: Jossey Bass, San Francisco.

Allan, J. 1989 *How to Develop Your Personal Management Skills*: Kogan Page, London.

Anderson, M., Chiriboga, D.A. and Bailey, J.T. 1988 Changes in management stressors on ICU nurses. *Dimensions of Critical Care Nursing*: 7: 2: 111–117.

Argyle, M. 1983 *The Psychology of Interpersonal Behaviour*: 4th Edition: Penguin, Harmondsworth.

Argyle, M. (ed.) 1981 *Social Skills and Health*: Methuen, London.

Argyris, C. and Schon, D. 1974 *Theory in Practice: Increasing Professional Effectiveness*: Jossey Bass, San Francisco.

Argyris, C. 1982 *Reasoning, Learning and Action*: Jossey Bass, San Francisco.

Arnold, E. and Boggs, K. 1989 *Interpersonal Relationships: Professional Communication Skills for Nurses*: Saunders, Philadelphia.

Arnold, M.B. 1984 *Memory and the Brain*: Lawrence Erlbaum Associates, Hillsdale, New Jersey.

Ashworth, P. 1987 Technology and machines – bad masters but good servants. *Intensive Care Nursing*: 3: 1: 1–2.

Astbury, C. 1988 *Stress in Theatre Nurses*: Royal College of Nursing, London.

Ausberger, D. 1979 *Anger and Assertiveness in Pastoral Care*: Fortress Press, Philadelphia.

Baddeley, D. 1983 *Your Memory: A User's Guide*: Penguin, Harmondsworth.

Baer, J. 1976 *How to Be Assertive (Not Aggressive): Women in Life, in Love and on the Job*: Signet, New York.

Bailey, R. 1985 *Coping With Stress in Caring*: Blackwell, Oxford.

Ball, M.J. and Hannah, K.J. 1984 *Using Computers in Nursing*: Reston Publishing, Reston, Virginia.

Baruth, L.G. 1987 *An Introduction to the Counselling Profession*: Prentice-Hall, Englewood Cliffs, New Jersey.

Belkin, G.S. 1984 *Introduction to Counselling*: Brown, Dubuque, Iowa.

Benner, P. and Wrubel, J. 1989 *The Primacy of Caring: Stress and Coping in Health and Illness*: Addison Wesley, Menlo Park.

Bibbings, J. 1987 The stress of working in intensive care: a look at the research. *Nursing*: 3: 15: 567–570.

Bond, M. and Kilty, J. 1986 *Practical Methods of Dealing With Stress*: 2nd Edition: Human Potential Research Project, University of Surrey, Guildford.

Boone, E.J., Shearon, R.W., White, E.E. and Associates 1980 *Serving Personal and Community Needs Through Adult Education*: Jossey Bass, San Francisco.

Boud, D. and Prosser, M.T. 1980 Sharing responsibility: staff–student cooperation in learning. *British Journal of Educational Technology*: 11: 1: 24–35.

Boud, D., Keogh, R. and Walker, M. 1985 *Reflection: Turning Experience into Learning*: Kogan Page, London.

Boud, D.J. (ed.) 1981 *Developing Student Autonomy in Learning*: Kogan Page, London.

Boud, D. (ed.) 1973 *Experiential Learning Techniques in Higher Education*: Human Potential Learning Project, University of Surrey, Guildford, Surrey.

Bower, S.A. and Bower, G.H. 1976 *Asserting Yourself*: Addison Wesley, Reading, Mass.

Boydel, E.M. and Fales, A.W. 1983 Reflective Learning: key to learning from experience. *Journal of Humanistic Psychology*: 23: 2: 99–117.

Bram, P.J. and Katz, L.F. 1989 A study of burnout in nurses working in hospice and hospital oncology settings. *Oncology Nursing Forum*: 16: 4: 555–560.

Brandes, D. and Phillips, R. 1984 *The Gamester's Handbook*: Vol. 2: Hutchinson, London.

Brookfield, S.D. 1986 *Understanding and Facilitating Adult Learning: A Comprehensive Analysis of Principles and Effective Practices*: Open University Press, Milton Keynes.

Brookfield, S.D. 1987 *Developing Critical Thinkers: Challenging Adults to Explore Alternative Ways of Thinking and Acting*: Open University Press, Milton Keynes.

Broome, A. 1990 *Managing Change*: Macmillan, London.

Brown, S.D. and Lent, R.W. (eds) 1984 *Handbook of Counselling Psychology*: Wiley, Chichester.

Brundage, D.H. and Mackeracher, D. 1980 *Adult Learning Principles and their Application to Program Planning*: Ministry of Education, Ontario.

Burnard, P. 1989 The nurse as non-conformist. *Nursing Standard*: 4: 1: 32–35.

Burnard, P. 1988 Preventing burnout. *Journal of District Nursing*: 7: 5: 9–10.

Burnard, P. 1990 Recording counselling in nursing. *Senior Nurse*: 10: 3: 26–27.

Burnard, P. 1990 Counselling the boss. *Nursing Times*: 86: 1: 58–59.

Burnard, P. 1990 Counselling in crises. *Journal of District Nursing*: 8: 7: 15–16.

Burnard, P. 1988 Stress and relaxation in health visiting. *Health Visitor*: 61: 9: 272.

Burnard, P. 1990 *Learning Human Skills: An Experimental Guide for Nurses*: 2nd Edition: Heinemann, Oxford.

Burnard, P. and Morrison, P. 1990 *Nursing Research in Action: Developing Basic Skills*: Macmillan, London.

Burnard, P. 1990 Learning to care for the spirit: *Nursing Standard*: 4: 18: 38–39.

Burnard, P. 1988 Coping with other people's emotions. *The Professional Nurse*: 4: 1: 11–14.

Burnard, P. and Morrison, P. 1989 Counselling attitudes in community psychiatric nurses. *Community Psychiatric Nursing Journal*: 9: 5: 26–29.

Burnard, P. 1987 Spiritual distress and the nursing response: theoretical considerations and counselling skills. *Journal of Advanced Nursing*: 12: 377–382.

Burnard, P. 1989 Exploring nurses' attitudes to AIDS. *The Professional Nurse*: 5: 2: 84–90.

Burnard, P. 1988 Searching for meaning. *Nursing Times*: 84: 37: 34–36.

Burnard, P. 1989 Counselling in surgical nursing. *Surgical Nurse*: 2: 5: 12–14.

Burnard, P. 1989 Exploring sexuality. *Journal of District Nursing*: 8: 4: 9–11.

Burnard, P. 1989 The 'Sixth Sense'. *Nursing Times*: 85: 50: 52–53.

Burnard, P. 1988 The spiritual needs of atheists and agnostics. *The Professional Nurse*: 4: 3: 130–132.

Burnard, P. 1988 AIDS and sexuality. *Journal of District Nursing*: 7: 2: 7–8.

Burnard, P. 1989 *Teaching Interpersonal Skills: An Experiential Handbook for Health Professionals*: Chapman and Hall, London.

Calnan, J. 1983 *Talking with Patients* Heinemann, London.

Campbell, A. 1984 *Paid to Care?*: SPCK, London.

Campbell, A.V. 1981 *Rediscovering Pastoral Care*: Darton, Longman and Todd, London.

Campbell, A. 1984 *Moderated Love*: SPCK, London.

Carkuff, R.R. 1969 *Helping and Human Relations: Vol. I: Selection and Training*: Holt, Rinehart and Winston, New York.

Carlisle, J. and Leary, M. 1982 Negotiating groups. In Payne, R. and Cooper, C. (eds) *Groups at Work*: Wiley, Chichester.

Carson, B.V. 1989 *Spiritual Dimensions of Nursing Practice*: W.B. Saunders, Philadelphia.

Charles, J. 1983 When carers crash. *Social Work Today*: 15: 12: 18–20.

Chene, A. 1983 The concept of autonomy in adult education: a philosophical discussion. *Adult Education Quarterly*: 32: 1: 38–47.

Chenevert, M. 1978 *Special Techniques in Assertiveness Training for Women in the Health Professions*: C.V. Mosby, St Louis.

Cianni-Surridge, M. and Horan, J. 1983 On the wisdom of assertive job-seeking behaviour. *Journal of Counselling Psychology*: 30: 209–214.

Clark, M. 1978 Meeting the needs of the adult learner: using non-formal education for social action. *Convergence*: XI: 3–4.

Clark, C. 1978 *Assertive Skills for Nurses*: Contemporary Publishing, Wakefield, Mass.

Claxton, G. 1984 *Live and Learn: An Introduction to the Psychology of Growth and Change in Everyday Life*: Harper and Row, London.

Clutterbuck, D. 1985 *Everybody Needs a Mentor: How To Further Talent Within an Organisation*: The Institute of Personnel Management, London.

Collins, G.C. and Scott, P. 1979 Everyone who makes it has a mentor. *Harvard Business Review*: 56: 89–101.

Cooper, C.L. and Payne, R. (eds) 1978 *Stress at Work*: Wiley, Chichester.

Corey, F. 1983 *I Never Knew I Had A Choice*: 2nd Edition: Brooks-Cole, California.

Cormier, L.S. 1987 *The Professional Counsellor: A Process Guide to Helping*: Prentice-Hall, Englewood Cliffs, New Jersey.

Cunningham, P.M. 1983. Helping Students Extract Meaning from Experience. In Smith, R.M. (ed.) *Helping Adults Learn How to Learn: New Directions for Continuing Education No 19*: Jossey Bass, San Francisco.

Curtis, L., Sturm, G., Billing, D.R. and Anderson, J.D. 1989 At the breaking point: when should an overworked nurse bail out? *Journal of Chistrian Nursing*: 6: 1: 4–9.

Daniels, V. and Horowitz, L.J. 1984 *Being and Caring: A Psychology for Living*: 2nd Edition: Mayfield, Mountain View, California.

Davis, C.M. 1981 Affective education for the health professions. *Physical Therapy*: 61: 11: 1587–1593.

de Bono, E. 1982 *de Bono's Thinking Course*: BBC, London.

De Vito, J.A. 1986 *The Interpersonal Communication Book*: 4th Edition: Harper and Row, New York.

deLeeuw, M. and de Leeuw, E. 1965 *Read Better Read Faster*: Penguin, Harmondsworth.

Dickson, A. 1985 *A Woman in Your Own Right: Assertiveness and You*: Quartet Books, London.

Distance Learning Centre 1986 *Stress in Nursing: An Open Learning Study Pack*: Distance Learning Centre, South Bank Polytechnic, London.

Dixon, D.N. and Glover, J.A. 1984 *Counselling: A Problem Solving Approach*: Wiley, Chichester.

Dobson, C.B. 1982 *Stress: The Hidden Anxiety*: MTP Press, Lancaster.

Dowd, C. 1983 Learning through experience. *Nursing Times*: 27th July: 50–52.

Dryden, W., Charles-Edwards, D. and Woolfe, R. 1989 *Handbook of Counselling in Britain*: Routledge, London.

Dusek, E.D. 1989 *Weight Management the Fitness Way: Exercise, Nutrition, Stress Control and Emotional Readiness*: Jones and Bartlett, London.

Edmunds, M. 1983 The nurse preceptor role: *Nurse Practitioner*: 8: 6: 52–53.

Egan, G. 1986 *Exercises in Helping Skills*: 3rd edition: Brooks/Cole, Monterey, California.

Ellis, R. (ed.) 1989 *Professional Competence and Quality Assurance in the Caring Professions*: Chapman and Hall, London.

Epting, F. 1984 *Personal Construct Counselling and Psychotherapy*: Wiley, Chichester.

Ernst, S. and Goodison, L. 1981 *In our Own Hands: A Book of Self Help Therapy*: The Womens' Press, London.

Evans, D. (ed.) 1990 *Why Should We Care?* Macmillan, London.

Farber, B.A. (ed.) 1983 *Stress and Burnout in the Human Services*: Pergamon Press, London.

Fernando, S. 1990 *Mental Health, Race and Culture*: Macmillan, London.

Ferruci, P. 1982 *What We May Be*: Turnstone Press, Wellingborough.

Fielding, P. and Berman, P. (eds) 1989 *Surviving in General Management*: Macmillan, London.

Filley, A.C. 1975 *Interpersonal Conflict Resolution*: Scott, Foresman, Glenview, Illinois.

Firth, H., McKeown, P., McIntee, J. and Britton, P. 1987 Burn-out, personality and support in long-stay nursing. *Nursing Times*: 83: 32: 55–57.

Fisher, R. and Ury, W. 1983 *Getting to Yes: Negotiating Agreement Without Giving In*: Hutchinson, London.

Fisher, S. and Reason, J. 1988 *Handbook of Life Stress: Cognition and Health*: Wiley, Chichester.

Fontana, D. 1989 *Managing Stress*: British Psychological Society and Routledge, London.

Frankl, V.E. 1959 *Man's Search for Meaning*: Beacon Press, New York.

Frankl, V.E. 1978 *The Unheard Cry for Meaning*: Simon and Schuster, New York.

Freeman, R. 1982 *Mastering Study Skills*: Macmillan, London.

Geller, L. 1985 Another look at self-actualisation. *Journal of Humanistic Psychology*: 24: 2: 93–106.

Gibbs, G. 1981 *Teaching Students to Learn*: Open University, Milton Keynes.

Glennerster, H. and Owens, P. 1990 *Nursing in Conflict*: Macmillan, London.

Goffman, I. 1971 *The Presentation of Self in Everyday Life*: Penguin, Harmondsworth.

Goldberg, L. and Beznitz, S. 1982 *Handbook of Stress: Theoretical and Clinical Aspects*: Macmillan, New York.

Halmos, P. 1965 *The Faith of the Counsellors*: Constable, London.

Hanks, L. Belliston, L. and Edwards, D. 1977 *Design Yourself*: Kaufman, Los Altos, California.

Hanson, P. 1986 *The Joy of Stress*: Pan, London.

Hargie, O. (ed.) 1987 *A Handbook of Communication Skills*: Croom Helm, London.

Hargie, O., Saunders, C. and Dickson, D. 1981 *Social Skills in Interpersonal Communication*: 2nd Edition Croom Helm, London.

Hawkins, P. and Shohet, R. 1989 *Supervision and the Helping Professions*: Open University Press, Milton Keynes.

Heginbotham, C. 1990 *Mental Health, Human Rights and Legislation*: Macmillan, London.

Herinck, R. (ed.) 1980 *The Psychotherapy Handbook*: New American Library, New York.

Heron, J. 1973 *Experiential Training Techniques*: Human Potential Research Project, University of Surrey, Guildford.

Heron, J. 1977 *Behaviour Analysis in Education and Training*: Human Potential Research Project, University of Surrey, Guildford.

Heron, J. 1978 *Co-Counselling Teachers Manual*: Human Potential Research Project, University of Surrey, Guildford.

Heron, J. 1980 *Paradigm Papers*: Human Potential Research Project, University of Surrey, Guildford.

Heywood-Jones, I. 1990 *The Nurse's Code: A Practical Approach to the Code of Professional Conduct*: Macmillan, London.

Heywood-Jones, I. 1989 *Helping Hands*: Macmillan, London.

Hill, S.S. and Howlett, H.A. 1988 *Success in Practical Nursing in Personal Vocational Issues*: W.B. Saunders, Philadelphia, PA.

Holt, R. 1982 An alternative to mentorship. *Adult Education*: 55: 2: 152–156.

Houle, C.O. 1984 *Patterns of Learning*: Jossey Bass, San Francisco.

Howard, K. and Sharp, J.A. 1983 *The Management of a Student Research Project*: Gower, Aldershot.

Howard, G.S., Nance, D.W. and Meyers, P. 1987 *Adaptive Counselling and Therapy: A Systematic Approach to Selecting Effective Treatments*: Jossey bass, San Francisco.

Hull, D. and Schroeder, H. 1979 Some Interpersonal Effects of Assertion, Non-Assertion and Aggression. *Behaviour Therapy*: 10: 20–29.

James, M. and Jongeward, D. 1971 *Born to Win: Transactional Analysis With Gestalt Experiments*: Addison-Wesley, Reading, Mass.

Jenkins, E. 1987 *Facilitating Self-Awareness: A Learning Package Combining Group work with Computer Assisted Learning*: Open Software Library, Wigan.

Johnson, D.W. 1972 *Reaching Out*: Prentice-Hall, Englewood Cliffs, New Jersey.

Jones, G. 1988 High-tech stress: identification and prevention. *Occupational Health*: 40: 9: 648–649.

Jung, C.G. 1976 *Modern Man in Search of a Soul*: Routledge and Kegan Paul, London.

Kelly, C. 1979 *Assertion Training: A Facilitator's Guide*: University Associates La Jolla, California.

Kennedy, E. 1979 *On Becoming a Counsellor*: Gill and Macmillan, London.

Kilty, J. 1987 *Staff Development for Nurse Education: Practitioners Supporting Students: A Report of a 5-Day Development Workshop*: Human Potential Research Project, University of Surrey, Guildford.

Kilty, J. 1978 *Self and Peer Assessment*: Human Potential Research Project, University of Surrey, Guildford.

King, E.C. 1984 *Affective Education in Nursing: A Guide to Teaching and Assessment*: Aspen, Maryland.

Kizer, W.M. 1987 *The Health Workplace: A Blueprint for Corporate Action*: Delmar, London.

Knowles, M.S. and Associates 1984 *Andragogy in Action: Applying Modern Principles of Adult Learning*: Jossey Bass, San Francisco.

Knowles 1978 *The Adult Learner: A Neglected Species*: 2nd Edition: Gulf, Texas.

Knowles, M. 1980 *The Modern Practice of Adult Education: From Pedagogy to Andragogy*: 2nd Edition: Follett, Chicago.

Knox, A.B. (ed.) 1980 *Teaching Adults Effectively*: Jossey Bass, San Francisco, California.

Koberg, D. and Bagnal, J. 1981 *The Revised All New Universal Traveller: A Soft-Systems Guide to Creativity, Problem-Solving and the Process of Reaching Goals*: Kaufmann, Los Altos, California.

Kopp, S. 1974 *If You Meet the Buddha on the Road, Kill Him!: A Modern Pilgrimage Through Myth, Legend and Psychotherapy*: Sheldon Press, London.

Lazarus, R.S. and Folkman, S. 1984 *Stress, Appraising and Coping*: Springer, New York.

Leech, K. 1986 *Spirituality and Pastoral Care*: Sheldon Press, London.

Lewis, H. and Streitfield, H. 1971 *Growth Games*: Bantam Books, New York.

Liberman, R.P., King, L.W., DeRisi, W.J. and McCann, M. 1976 *Personal Effectiveness*: Research Press, Champagne, Illinois.

Madders, J. 1980 *Stress and Relaxation*: Martin Dunitz, London.

Marcer, D. 1986 *Biofeedback and Related Therapies in Clinical Practice*: Chapman and Hall, London.

Marshall, E.K. and Kurtz, P.D. (eds) 1982 *Interpersonal Helping Skills: A Guide to Training Methods, Programs and Resources*: Jossey bass, San Francisco.

Marson, S. (ed.) 1990 *Managing People*: Macmillan, London.

May, K.M. et al. 1982 Mentorship for scholarliness: opportunities and dilemmas. *Nursing Outlook*: 30: 22–28.

Meichenbaum, D. 1983 *Coping With Stress*: Century Publishing, London.

Meyeroff, M. 1972 *On Caring*: Harper and Row, New York.

Mezeiro, J. 1981 A critical theory of adult learning and education. *Adult Education*: 32: 1: 3–24.

Michelson, L., Sugari, D., Wood, R. and Kazadin, A. 1983 *Social Skills Assessment and Training with Children*: Plenum Press, New York.

Milne, D., Burdett, C. and Beckett, J. 1986 Assessing and reducing the stress and strain of psychiatric nursing. *Nursing Times*: 82: 19: 59–62.

Morley, I.E. 1982 Preparation for negotiating: conflict, commitment and choice. In Bradstatter, H., Davis, J.H. and Stocker-Kreichgauer, G. (eds) *Group Decision Making*: Academic Press, London.

Morley, I.E. 1987 Negotiating and bargaining. In Hargie, O. (ed.) *A Handbook of Communication Skills*: Croom Helm, London.

Morton-Cooper, A. 1989 *Returning to Nursing: A Guide for Nurses and Health Visitors*: Macmillan, London.

Murgatroyd, S. and Woolfe, R. 1982 *Coping with Crisis – Understanding and Helping Persons in Need*: Harper and Row, London.

Murgatroyd, S. 1986 *Counselling and Helping*: British Psychological Society and Methuen, London.

Murphy, L.R. 1984 Occupational stress management: a review and appraisal. *Journal of Occupational Psychology*: 57: 1–15.

Nadler, L. (ed) 1984 *The Handbook of Human Resource Development*: Wiley, New York.

Nash, E.S. 1989 Occupational stress and the oncology nurse. *Nursing*: 4: 8: 37–38.

Nelson-Jones, R. 1988 *Practical Counselling and Helping Skills: Helping Clients to Help Themselves*: Cassell, London.

Nelson-Jones, R. 1984 *Personal Responsibility: Counselling and Therapy: An Integrative Approach*: Harper and Row, London.

Nelson, M.J. 1989 *Managing Health Professionals*: Chapman and Hall, London.

Nichols, K. and Jenkinson, J. 1990 *Leading a Support Group*: Chapman and Hall, London.

Nierenberg, G.I. 1973 *Fundamentals of Negotiation*: Hawthorn, New York.

Open University Coping with Crisis Group 1987 Running Workshops: *A Guide for Trainers in the Helping Professions*: Croom Helm, London.

Payne, R. and Firth-Cozens, J. 1987 *Stress in Health Professionals*: Wiley, Chichester.

Peplau, H.E. 1988 *Interpersonal Relationships in Nursing*: Macmillan, London.

Phelps, S. and Austin, N. 1975 *The Assertive Woman*: Impact, San Luis Obispo, California.

Porritt, L. 1990 *Interaction Strategies: An Introduction for Health Professionals*: 2nd Edition: Churchill Livingstone, Edinburgh.

Postman, N. and Weingartner, C.W. 1969 *Teaching as a Subversive Activity*: Penguin, Harmondsworth.

Rankin-Box, D.F. 1987 *Complementary Health Therapies: A Guide for Nurses and the Caring Professions*: Chapman and Hall, London.

Reddy, M. 1987 *The Manager's Guide to Counselling at Work*: Methuen, London.

Rogers, C.R. 1983 *Freedom to Learn for the Eighties*: Merrill, Columbus.

Rogers, C.R. and Stevens, B. 1967 *Person to Person: The Problem of Being Human*: Real People Press. Lafayette, California.

Rowan, J. 1986 Holistic listening. *Journal of Humanistic Psychology*: 26: 1: 83–102.

Roy, I. 1973 *Structural Integration*: Viking Press, New York.

Russell, P. 1979 *The Brain Book*: Routledge and Kegan Paul, London.

Scammell, B. 1990 *Communication Skills*: Macmillan, London.

Schafer, B.P. and Morgan, M.K. 1980 An experiential learning laboratory: a new dimension in teaching mental health skills. *Issues in Mental Health Nursing*: 2: 3: 47–57.

Schmidt, J.A. and Wolfe, J.S. 1980 The mentor partnership: discovery of professionalism. *NASPA Journal*: 17: 45–51.

Scott, W.P. 1981 *The Skills of Negotiating*: Gower, Aldershot.

Scott, W.P. 1986 *The Skills of Communicating*: Gower, Aldershot.

Shafer, P. 1978 *Humanistic Psychology*: Prentice-Hall, Englewood Cliffs, New Jersey.

Simon, S.B., Howe, L.W. and Kirschenbaum, H. 1978 *Values Clarification*: Revised Edition: A and W Visual Library, New York.

Skevington, S. (ed.) 1984 *Understanding Nurses: The Social Psychology of Nursing*: Wiley, Chichester.

Smith, S. and Smith, C. 1990 *Personal Health Choices*: Jones and Bartlett, London.

Smith, E. and Wilks, N. 1988 *Meditation*: Macdonald, London.

Speizer, J.J. 1981 Role models, mentors and sponsors: the elusive concept. *Signs*: 6: 692–712.

Stanfield, P. 1990 *Introduction to Health Professions*: 2nd Edition: Jones and Bartlett, London.

Strauss, A. 1978 *Negotiations: Varieties, Contexts and Social Order*: Jossey Bass, San Francisco.

Sudman, S. and Bradburn, N.M. 1982 *Asking Questions: A Practical Guide to Questionnaire Design*: Jossey Bass, San Francisco.

Sweeney, M.A. 1985 *The Nurses Guide to Computers*: Macmillan, New York.

Tanner, D. 1986 *That's Not What I Meant!: How Conversational Style Makes or Breaks Your Relations with Others*: Dent, London.

The Professional Nurse Developments Series 1990 *Effective Communication*: Austen Cornish, London.

The Professional Nurse Developments Series 1990 *The Ward Sister's Survival Guide*: Austen Cornish, London.

The Professional Nurse Developments Series 1990 *Practice Check!*: Austen Cornish, London.

The Professional Nurse Developments Series 1990 *The Staff Nurse's Survival Guide*: Austen Cornish, London.

The Professional Nurse Developments Series 1990 *Patient Education Plus*: Austen Cornish, London.

Thompson, J. 1989 Stress sense. *Nursing Times*: 85: 21: 20.

Thygerson, A. 1989 *Fitness and Health: Lifestyle Strategies*: Jones and Bartlett, London.

Torrington, D. 1982 *Face-To-Face in Management*: Prentice-Hall, Englewood Cliffs, New Jersey.

Totton, N. and Edmonston, E. 1988 *Reichian Growth Work: Melting the Blocks to Life and Love*: Prism Press, Bridport.

Trower, P. (ed.) 1984 *Radical Approaches to Social Skills Training*: Croom Helm, London.

Tschudin, V. 1986 *Counselling Skills for Nurses*: Balliere Tindall, London.

Tshudin, V. and Schober, J. 1990 *Managing Yourself*: Macmillan, London.

Wallis, R. 1984 *Elementary Forms of the New Religious Life*: Routledge and Kegan Paul, London.

Watkins, J. 1978 *The Therapeutic Self*: Human Science Press, New York.

Wlodkowski, R.J. 1985 *Enhancing Adult Motivation to Learn*: Jossey Bass, San Francisco.

Woodward, J. 1988 *Understanding Ourselves: The Uses of Therapy*: Macmillan, London.

Zajonc, R. 1980 Feelings and thinking: preferences need no interference. *American Psychologist*: 35: 151–175.

Index of Exercises

Index